a page in the life

a page in the life

true life stories from RTÉ's
THE MARIAN FINUCANE SHOW

edited by CLAIRE PRIOR

NEW
ISLAND

a page in the life
First published 2005
by New Island
2 Brookside
Dundrum Road
Dublin 14
www.newisland.ie

ISBN 1 904301 95 9

British Library Cataloguing in Publication Data. A CIP catalogue
record for this book is available from the British Library.

Typeset by New Island
Cover design by Fidelma Slattery @ New Island
Printed in the UK by Cox & Wyman

10 9 8 7 6 5 4 3 2 1

The Irish Hospice Foundation supports the
development of access to hospice care in Ireland.

The Irish Hospice Foundation
Morrison Chambers
32 Nassau Street
Dublin 2

Phone: 01 6793188 Email: info@hospice-foundation.ie
www.hospice-foundation.ie

CONTENTS

Acknowledgments — xi

Foreword — Marian Finucane — xiii

The Knockout — Robert Barrett — 1

False Starts — Helen Dwyer — 4

Circle Time — Cyril Kelly — 7

The Affair — Anonymous — 10

Nostalgia — David Berkeley — 13

The Dating Game — Claire Mullan — 16

Any Developments? — Fiachra Kennedy — 19

Naked Reunion — Alison Lyons — 22

Chance Encounter — Colm Nolan — 25

Far from Home — Annette Poro — 28

A Horse Story — Peter Keogh — 31

I Wish I Was in Dixie — Aoife Ní Oistín — 34

The Pleasure Dog — Declan McHugh — 37

One August Morning — Ciara Considine — 40

Cusack's Last Stand — Sean O'Callaghan — 43

Nits — Winifred Power — 46

Coming Home — Mary Hayward — 49

Memories of Another Life — Eddie Naughton — 51

Twenty-first Century Romance — Anne Waterson — 54

The Graveyard — Linda Richardson — 57

Shiny Things — Ailish Connelly — 60

Real Life — Joseph Sweeney — 63

The New House — Letizia Aresu — 66

What Do You Know? — Mags Treanor — 69

I Will Never Find Love — Orla Martin — 72

Canvassing — Michael McLoughlin — 74

Hard to Swallow — Anonymous — 77

Coffee at Eleven — Fiona Marshall — 80

Valentine Record — Mary Cooke — 84

Suspicion — Tim Cronin — 87

The Things You Believe — Aoife Duggan — 90

A Run-in With St Brigid — Jane O'Rourke — 95

How the World Works — Joe Phelan — 98

New Man — Joan Hannon — 101

Salsa Class: Beginners — Sheila Killian — 104

The Readers — Michael Thurlow — 107

Derby and Me — Ger Petrie — 111

The Staff Do — Cathy Sweeney — 114

The Bedsit — Trish Byrne — 117

While They Are Retired — Anonymous — 120

Old Brown Eyes — Anne Molloy — 123

The Small Town — Carole Zabbal — 126

Bread — Jim Clarken — 129

The Mouths of Babes — Mary Barber — 132

To Oz and Back — Sharon Vogiatzi — 135

Cowardice — L. Hingerty — 138

The Key — Margaret McCarthy — 140

The Gallery — Michael Minihan — 142

Night into Morning — Sheila Maher — 144

The Student Party — Dylan Bradley — 147

The Salon — Helen Delaney — 149

Observations — Myles Christian — 152

The Journey — Mary McGregor — 155

The End of the Day — D. Woods — 158

ACKNOWLEDGMENTS

Thanks to all those whose support made this
book possible: Eithne Hand, John McMahon,
Sinead Mooney and the *Marian Finucane*
programme team. Thanks also to Brian
Thunder and Clodagh O'Donoghue, whose
voices brought the stories to life on air
throughout the year.

FOREWORD

Sometimes on the radio programme you do something that strikes a chord with people in the most extraordinary way. That was what happened with 'A Page in the Life'. Last year we invited our listeners to write stories that reflected their lives in today's Ireland. Not an epic, just about 500 words that expressed a sense of themselves and their place in the world. We asked that they be 'contemporary, Irish and true'.

The stories flooded in by post and by email: stories of births and of deaths, of loves won and lost, of small events which had a lasting impact and quiet moments of epiphany.

Throughout the year the stories continued to flow, many from people who told us they'd never written anything before. In all we received well over a thousand entries; just 54 were read on air during the programme. Those 54 stories are presented here, together for the first time, in all their diversity.

It's important to me that the royalties from the book will go to the Irish Hospice

Foundation. It's a charity whose work we celebrated in a special programme this year marking the annual Coffee Morning for Hospice fundraiser, with which I have been involved over many years. These stories give us an insight into how we live our lives and the Irish Hospice Foundation, perhaps more than any other organisation, understands that life is for living, right to the very end.

Finally thanks to all the authors who wrote to us for sharing their stories with us. I hope you enjoyed writing them as much as we have hearing them. Perhaps this book will encourage more of us to capture moments from our lives on paper. We all have 'A Page in the Life' worth sharing.

Marian Finucane
August 2005

the knockout

ROBERT BARRETT

I don't drink coffee but I have now ingested several litres of it and my heart is a galloping racehorse. I rub my blood-shot eyes and cling desperately to this racehorse's tail. It is the morning of the second night without sleep and as the sun rises through the window our giddiness is turning to panic. This is the real thing. There is no way back.

A grey-haired, middle-aged man with unlaced shoes enters the room. He wears the grumpiness of a man roused from his bed.

Needle in hand, he mumbles earnest instructions and I leap to attention. He is an expert. Had he told me to open the window and jump out through it, I'd be there now, splattered onto the car-park. The nurse has a French accent and her perfect bouffant bobs as she dispenses order to chaos. We're getting close now. I am sent to the corner like a scolded child to keep an eye on, 'ze heart monitooor'. It is fine before I go near it, but somehow feeding off my panic, it is soon flying up and down like the seismograph at the epicentre of an earthquake. I go back to fetching tissues and glasses of water.

The French nurse calls the midwife and Houdini breezes through the door. Her bright beatific smile lights the room. 'My third of the day!' she says. She is charged up on the pure energy of birthing babies and eats self-doubt for breakfast. The sleeves are rolled up and the real business begins. I hear my own words of encouragement and realise that I am a man in a room of grannies sucking eggs. I watch the monitor, fetch a glass of water (drink it all myself), fetch another glass, hold hands, rub arms and shout nonsensical, bungling words of encouragement.

After twenty minutes, Houdini produces the object of our labours. I am called forward out of the wilderness of water-fetching and monitor-watching to cut the rubbery cord. My wife and I communicate our delight with laughter and shock. After nine months of hard work, she is exhausted, out of breath, ecstatic with her first baby. She wonders what to do next.

In a few minutes, Houdini hands me a blue ball of cotton-wrapped, bawling noise. The bundle is lighter than I could believe and the crying is louder than I could imagine. I wonder what to do next. Nobody comes to tell me. This is serious. I slump down in a chair with my blue cotton bundle and the 'Greatest Moments' video recorder in my head begins to record automatically; thankfully so, because I am somewhere else, socked in the jaw, and knocked-out by the beauty of life.

false starts

HELEN DWYER

I hope she will like me. I hope she's not a bag lady or a wino. I couldn't deal with that. I wonder if she's nervous too.

The seconds dawdle through the tension. I feel small and scared, like I'm facing my first day at school. I hope for so much from meeting her: the answers to all my questions, the answer to ... A lot to ask of her. Too much as it transpires. But for now I wait under the town-hall clock.

She said three o'clock. What if she's late?

What if we don't recognise each other? This could be a big mistake …

I hope she looks like me. Jesus, someone, somewhere has got to look like me.

Three o'clock chimes, startling me out of my mixture of hope and dread. Time seems to freeze. The clouds seem to park overhead. A lifetime of waiting has led me here. A lifetime of hope and dread. She can't be late and make me wait even longer; that would be too cruel.

I'm bound to be disappointed – my hopes are too high for the real world. I expect a happy ending but this is no fairy-tale.

This might be her … she's tall and blond like me. Very good looking, maybe too good looking. She walks past without a glance in my direction.

More waiting. She's late now, if she's coming at all. A whole minute passes. An old shabby woman steps out of the rushing crowd. She touches my arm. I freeze.

'Do you have any spare change?'

'Sure.'

I give her whatever coins I have. She blends back into the crowd. I wait.

Then I see her approaching. She has my looks, or rather, I have hers. I know her and she knows me. She is not a bag lady or a wino, but a well-dressed country lady with

gold jewellery. She reaches out to hug me —
too close too soon. We shake hands instead.
Skin to skin again.

Tears glitter in her eyes. I fight back my
own tears. Our eyes meet. Her hand in mine
is small and cold. She is not the mother I
dreamed of. She is a small, frightened, weeping old lady.

circle time

CYRIL KELLY

'Circle Time', the manual claimed, was the new panacea for the ills besetting education today. It would enhance pupils' self-esteem, improve class morale, even arouse empathy in the most disaffected little macho man around. So, what was I waiting for?

My first difficulty was to get my lads to sit in a circle on the floor. It wasn't so much the geometric concept that presented a problem, more the social notion. Mickser wouldn't sit near Seamaí, Marko's sister had dumped Philly and Chilly's da had moved in with Mushroom's ma the previous week. Eventually, after I'd cajoled and counselled, we were ready.

I was going around the restless circle with my saucer of sweets, proffering one to any fellow who said something positive either about himself or a classmate. But by the time they had learned that 'boastfulness' was not the same as 'saying something positive', it was nearly home time.

Out of the blue, Ghosty, the smallest, quietest fellow in the class, spoke. He just wanted to know could we get a class pet? All differences and dissent were immediately forgotten. Before I could intervene, some lads had a horse bought in Smithfield and had him grazing at the back of the school. Another lad's neighbour had snakes while someone's culchie cousin had found a fox cub. But the reality came down to a choice between goldfish, pigeons or mice. An amazingly adult discussion ensued. All about care, cost and commitment. The bell was long gone when a consensus was arrived at — mice it was. By unanimous choice Ghosty was given the responsibility of collecting fifty cent from everybody and making the purchase.

On Monday morning our two sniffing, darting, defecating, pink-eyed orphans arrived. I had just placed their cage on the press and was calling the roll when Sparky declared that the mice should have names as well. Thinking I was being smart, I wondered aloud about their gender – a boy mouse wouldn't want a Miss Mousy name. Suddenly the place was like the pit in Wall Street. Everybody knew somebody who knew somebody who knew what to look for. When I got peace restored Ghosty said that, in the pet shop, Waxy had explained everything.

With a nod from myself and gleeful urgings from the lads, Ghosty went to the cage and removed one of the mice. Grasping each hind leg between finger and thumb, a minute scrutiny was carried out beneath the frenzied tail. 'A boy!' Ghosty announced, returning the squealing creature and grab-bing his companion. Almost immediately, a similar verdict: another boy! So we christ-ened them Eminem and Rap.

On the following Thursday morning, Sparky was cleaning out the cage when he gave a screech. 'Sir! Sir!' In the corner he had discovered half a dozen new-born mice. In these days of sex education and 'exploring masculinities', with controversy raging among parents and teachers, I reckoned that it was time to revise the biological basics with my lads.

the affair

ANONYMOUS

I should be used to it by now. The tension that morning. The fear that this time one of the lies will trip me up. That this time I will be caught. All morning my heart is pounding. I get no work done. I am deliberately vague about an afternoon meeting when I leave the office. 'I'm on the mobile!' I call out to no one in particular and I'm gone.

I look as always. Business suit. High heels. But today I am wearing my best Jo Malone body crème. Matching fragrance. New lingerie. Stockings – always stockings.

Lunch will be discreet. One of our usual bistros. A kiss on the cheek when I arrive. A lingering look that betrays the sweet anticipation of the afternoon ahead. We will talk work, politics, kids – just like every other diner. Occasionally he will touch my hand when reaching for the water. Or he will stroke the back of my neck when helping me on with my coat. I will brush off his leg when crossing mine under the table.

Delicious foreplay.

We will leave and go separate ways. I will drive to the hotel. Park my car in the underground car-park and check in at reception. A false name, obviously. Paying cash to avoid using my credit card. I hate that part. I'm sure I look suspicious. One day someone I know will walk in just as I am checking into a hotel room at 2.30 on a Tuesday afternoon. But not today. She hands me the keycard and enquires about my luggage. 'It's in the car,' I say. 'I'll bring it up later.' Then up to the room. Order the champagne. Text him the room number. And wait …

A knock on the door. Finally. 'Hey you,' he says. I smile. For three hours I think of nothing – not kids, not housework, not spreadsheets, not traffic, not team meetings, not what to make for dinner, not the visa bill, not homework, not world poverty, not don't forget the dry cleaning. Nothing. But this. This incredible, fantastic, amazing sex. Oh, wonderful, glorious, divine sex. Not married-Saturday-night-kids-in-the-next-room sex. But this. Erotic, exhausting, explosive Hollywood sex. Wave after wave of pleasure, exquisite pleasure flooding through my veins.

5.30 p.m. Should be gone. A quick shower and a long kiss goodbye. 'See you next month,' he says. 'Absolutely,' I say. It's always worth it.

Into the traffic. Rush hour. Quick call. 'I'm running late,' I say. 'My meeting ran over. And now the traffic is murder. Any chance you could pick up the kids?'

nostalgia

DAVID BERKELEY

I used to think that nostalgia was for solace and entertainment in old age, but not any more. Recently I decided to re-visit the old Victorian shipwreck of my boyhood, stuck in the mud a few hundred yards offshore at the bottom of our road. Now only its ribs are left. My wife said she was not going to be left out of this adventure.

Having scanned the paper for tides, the sky for rain and our wellies for leaks, we drove to the spot and parked the car close to the shore. The wreck beckoned us, looking almost as of old. After testing the seabed for firmness we took a bearing on the hull and set off. As we picked our way among the stones the nostalgia began to wash over me. Crabs scuttled for shelter in the seaweed and reminded me of how I had tormented them when I was eight years old. I recalled reefing my hand on a broken bottle at the bottom when swimming underwater and seeing my blood on the surface when I came up, just like in *Jaws*.

In my growing excitement I failed to notice how soft the mud was getting. Comments like 'Are you sure this is a good idea?' from my wife were met with disdain. Our legs were showing a tendency to vacate our wellies and heavy dollops of mud were sticking to the boots. We were only thirty yards from the wreck. It seemed a shame, a defeat, not to carry on. The tide was still well out. I looked back at the shore and all seemed well. People were going about their business as if they expected us to do the same.

'Maybe the ground is firmer ahead,' I said weakly, as I leaned on my wife's shoulder to extract my left boot from the mud.

'Oh, yeah!' she replied, and I pulled out the right boot, causing the left one to sink even further.

I was sure Scott of the Antarctic would

not have given up so close to the Pole. I looked at the shore again, hoping to see worried people waving to us but no – they were still scurrying about, unconcerned. Suddenly I had a vision of the newspaper headlines – 'Elderly Couple in Suicide Pact'. I panicked.

'Maybe we should head back,' my wife said. As I had no better idea and she was so calm, I decided to use her shoulder again. After all, if she hadn't come, she might have lost me. So, step by sucking step, we made our way back. This time I ignored the scuttling crabs and the ancient itch in my reefed hand. Somehow all the romance was gone.

I almost kissed the car. As we drove home I wondered if we might try it again someday with snow shoes. But I suppose that would be cheating.

the dating game

CLAIRE MULLAN

I don't like to admit it but, let's face it, I'm desperate. I'm thirty-seven years old and I'm single. I've been waiting for Mr Right to turn up but it hasn't happened, so recently I decided to try shopping for a man on the Internet. I paid €9.95 to join a dating web site for a month. I stipulated that I'm looking for a man who is around my age, is single, doesn't smoke and lives in the same part of the country as I do. In no time I got messages from men – men in their fifties, men who are married with kids, men who smoke and men who live in England. My searches of the database weren't coming up with much either. I would have to relax my criteria. I made a short list of three and got into conversations with them through the web site and then exchanged phone numbers with them all.

Last week I met guy number one. Since he's single and living in the same town, I was prepared to overlook his smoking. He likes the theatre so we agreed to go to a play and then for a drink afterwards. Looks-wise he was no great shakes but we had plenty to talk about and got on well. Or at least we got on well until his sixth pint, when he started to get all horny and kept telling me that he wanted to take me to bed right now. He kept kissing me, or rather biting my lips, which he seemed to think I might enjoy, and wasn't hearing me when I told him I didn't want to do this. I walked away from him in disgust.

On to guy number two, a musician who plays guitar in pubs, separated, doesn't smoke. He lives halfway across the country but was going to be in my town to do some recording so we arranged to meet in a pub. He sounded really nice on the phone, all embarrassed and nervous but very down-to-earth. I had high hopes for him. I turned up at 9:30 p.m. but he wasn't there. At 9:45 I sent him a text just in case we were both there but missing each other. No reply. At ten I ordered another drink. At 10:25 a man in his sixties sat beside me and offered to buy me dinner – no strings, he promised. I tried to be polite and listen to his patronising 'you're a beautiful woman and that guy doesn't deserve you' speech but after five minutes I couldn't take any more and I left.

That leaves guy number three. I haven't decided whether to meet him or not. He has loads in common with me, all the same interests and hobbies and a similar outlook on life. We talked easily on the phone for ages. The trouble is he's fifty-four. It just seems too old.

I guess it's back to the drawing board.

any developments?

FIACHRA KENNEDY

'So, any developments?' I ask.

'No,' she replies.

'How many days is it now?'

'Seven.'

I pause. Then I mumble something about statistics, a huge percentage miscarry in the first month. Can never tell. Too early in the day. Might just be late. No point in getting too excited.

I'm sure she laughs to herself. Here he goes again. Always trying to dampen expectations. Wait for it now, here it comes, his own special mantra, 'Things will happen when they happen,' always spoken in that serious, weighty tone that he adopts.

But you see I am getting excited. Can't stop myself.

At night-time, I lie awake in bed day-dreaming about playing out in the back garden of our not-quite-purchased house. Of a small hand holding mine as we cross the road to the newsagent's to buy ice-cream. Of a small brown curly-haired head, drooping sleepily by the fire just before the woodcutter rescues Miss Little Red Hood and her seven merry men from the giant with the beanstalk. I'm still a bit sketchy on the details.

Of course, I know it'll change my life. Have to get up a little bit earlier, even at weekends. Have to drive from home to crèche to work to crèche to home. Have to stand on pitch-sides shouting encourage-ment and at the same time identify the parent of that hurley-wielding lunatic to have a quiet word about them exercising control over their little darling. Have to check spellings and tables. Have to worry about why they are still running a tem-perature, why they won't eat carrots, why they aren't home yet, why they haven't got their phone switched on, why they looked at me that way before slamming the door shut, why they haven't called or visited for weeks. These aren't really things I have to do; these are things I hope to do.

The phone rings.

'So,' I ask, 'any developments?'

'Yes,' she replies.

'…Well, there's always next month.'

naked reunion

ALISON LYONS

'Just hold on in here, please. I'll fetch the class from upstairs,' said the young, denim-clad art teacher, evading my eyes and motioning me towards a screen from which hung a dressing-gown.

I looked about the Georgian room. It had high ceilings and had probably once been elegant, but now its walls were covered with doodles and scribbles of charcoal, paint and pencil that gave the whole an extremely scruffy appearance. The floor was wooden and equally besmirched with 'art'. In the centre, ominously, stood a large wooden platform, not unlike an inverted sheep pen, which I guessed would be supporting me in all my naked glory in minutes to come. Large wooden easels were placed variously about the room, waiting for their owners. They'd come soon enough, cackling and clattering their way into the room. This was the calm before the storm.

My little corner consisted of the screen, the robe and a plastic chair. Presumably I was to furtively undress and then hide behind these hinged pieces of chipboard, only to emerge when called upon. I wasn't quite sure at what point I was to drop my coverings – presumably I'd be told. Whether to do it seductively, timidly or methodically I was as yet undecided. By now I was gripped by giddiness and more than a little hysteria.

At least I looked a hell of a lot better than I felt. I was in full make up – I figured that at least my face could remain masked throughout. They couldn't take that away from me. My lipstick was a rich red colour which, combined with my extremely white complexion, made me look a little like a blonde geisha. The purple dragon-embroidered dressing-gown completed the look.

I found myself checking my hair in my

small compact mirror. I suppose no one wants to be rejected – especially not by a gang of thirty people all at once. I also threw a last look down the length of my body. It was tweezed, exfoliated and moisturised, and fully waxed – except for what modesty demanded I leave. I figured that if I went without lunch and made an effort to hold it all in, I could keep my stomach relatively flat to all appearances.

The tutor had left a folder on the table just inside the room. Casually I flicked it open. It was a pictorial list of everyone in the class, a rogue's gallery of the sublime and the ridiculous. I was horrified to find a face that was very familiar to me. And there was his name. The boyfriend I'd had back home, at sixteen. And he was just about to be reunited with me after nine years, in the most singular of ways.

chance encounter

COLM NOLAN

One of my favourite things to do is grab a quiet moment, order a pot of tea and read the newspaper in the local coffee shop. As I went in to do just that last Saturday, I noticed someone was sitting in my usual spot, so I went down the back near the gilt-edged mirror and sat in the one remaining seat. The person in the seat opposite me had their back to me as I walked down and it was only when I sat down that I realised we knew each other. We had been at school together.

We said our hellos and I silently cursed my luck. He looked well, but now, like me, had a bit more weight and a lot less hair. I told him I was married with three kids and we spoke about how life now revolves around the children and their activities. He told me that just recently he had separated from his wife. As I listened to him talking about it I realised how lucky I am. He said he is now trying to rebuild his life, has moved into an apartment and is getting used to cooking for himself.

He said that he finds the weekends the hardest. Because he gets the kids every second weekend he says he feels the need to treat them. So he brings them shopping to Liffey Valley, then maybe the cinema and after that a meal. As he spoke of the emptiness inside him on Sunday nights I noticed his eyes misting. It's the hardest part, he said. He said he always plans to do some work on the Sunday night because 'if I don't I will open a bottle of wine'. I asked him what had happened that led to the separation. He replied that he still searches for the answer to that question.

'I am not a big drinker; we were both faithful to each other. I think we lost respect for each other,' he said. 'I was working very hard, so was she. The kids came along and we seemed to drift. Maybe we didn't take enough time for ourselves. We were very focused on getting the house right, making enough money to have nice cars, the right holidays. The rows got more frequent. Counselling didn't work, so I offered to move out, not thinking she would say yes. It was only when I spent the first week alone that the realiastion of what had happened hit me. Part of me was delighted; I felt a freedom, not to act like a single man, but a freedom from the bitterness and anger. The other part of me felt crushed.' He told me he spent the first month crying, that the only thing that kept him sane was work.

My mobile phone rang and he looked at his watch. I finished my brief call. Walking out we shook hands and he gave me his business card.

far from home

ANNETTE PORO

Jack, not yet two, smiles his sunshine smile at Sheila. 'Bye bye, Mama,' he waves and attempts to climb, head first, into the washing machine in her kitchen in Crumlin.

The Albanian Prime Minister is talking excitedly about infrastructure. He is interrupted every few seconds by a sound like an exotic bird in a nervous state. 'It's Billy Birdie,' Sheila says to Jack. When the bird screeches, so does Jack, and the Prime Minister turns fluorescent green. There is something seriously wrong with the satellite. Or rather with the receiver under the TV. Sheila knows that the problem is caused by Petit Filous in the works, but this insight has not been shared with her Albanian husband, Arben. She knows that satellite TV is as important to him as air and water.

Today, Sheila is under instruction not to turn off the TV until Arben returns, for fear the fragile signal will disappear entirely. This daft idea betrays his state of excitement. Tonight Albania plays Greece. Like Ireland playing England. Red jerseys emblazoned with black eagles are laid out on the couch. There is even a small jersey for Jack, sent from Tirana for the occasion. This time they will see Albania beat Greece, if only the exotic-bird problem can be eliminated.

At six o'clock, Arben returns with an expensive-looking new receiver under his arm. Still wearing his coat, he dives under the stairs for his toolbox. Within minutes the crowded stadium in Tirana appears clearly on the screen. No fluorescent green flashes, no screeching. The pre-match commentary has begun. Arben scans the faces in the crowd to see if he recognises anyone. 'Alexander should be there,' he tells Sheila, 'and Ilir.'

Marko and Bashkim arrive, dressed in red

and black, big good-looking men who, like Arben, cannot sit down with excitement. Jack tears around the room in his small jersey. His sandy Irish hair is dishevelled on his broad Albanian head. As the match begins, the atmosphere is so tense that Sheila is almost afraid to speak. When Jack stands in front of the screen, everyone roars. Then, an Albanian goal, and the men with the black eagles on their chests are close to crying with excitement. Half time, Albania ahead. The dream is unfolding as it was meant to. The men are hugging each other.

Suddenly, a gust outside and a loud metallic crash. The cheering sea of red and black on the screen is gone, replaced by a silent grey flicker. The men stare in stunned horror for a second. Then they return to life and curse wild Albanian curses. They run to thump the TV into action. Arben runs outside. Everyone follows him. Jack shouts 'Daddy, Babi,' and dashes barefoot into the garden where the satellite dish is lying bent and broken on the concrete path. Slowly and silently they retreat into the house and stare again into the grey abyss. Nobody speaks. 'Birdie gone,' Jack says.

a horse story

PETER KEOGH

Courtown, Wexford, 2001. The Keogh brothers and partners are sunning themselves for a couple of weeks, boosted by the news that they've both just had the winner of the English Grand National. Red Marauder has romped home at thirty-three to one and ensured that the Keogh brigade will have a holiday to remember. The last two furlongs were the topic of heated conversation as we swaggered down the main street. Tom insists that the jockey should have stayed on the rails and not tried to go around the outside; Peter, the wise, tries to explain that the horse could have been boxed in if he hadn't gone around the slower nags.

This conversation jumped back and forth as kebabs were munched and tactical decisions were discussed. Then suddenly, Tom decides that he wants to go horse riding so he can show us exactly how the winning jockey should have ridden the winning horse.

A passer by was stopped and directions asked for a horse. After much laughter our new friend pointed us further down the road and off we trotted.

Our horse was duly found. While not being the biggest beast in the world, Tom assures us that size isn't everything, as his wife chokes on her kebab. Tom mounts the beast, feet are placed in the stirrups and reins tightly grasped, money is paid and Tom proceeds to gently nudge Gala along.

While sitting in the jockey stance and rocking back and forth Tom explains how the jockey should have pushed his way through along the rails. But as Gala starts to speed up Tom's foot slips out of the stirrup. Amid much nervous laughter from the brigade Tom grabs Gala's neck and tries to get his foot back into the stirrup. Gala is now heading for home and has broken into what could be described as a gallop. Slowly Tom's grip around Gala's neck starts to slip and he starts to slide from the horse – the brigade at this stage have forgotten their kebabs and are furiously searching handbags for cameras. A crowd has now gathered and are shouting words of encouragement to Tom.

With one foot still in the stirrup Tom finally loses his grip and falls from the horse, landing heavily on the ground. Tom is now blubbering and not half as brave as he was five minutes ago. Gala keeps going and Tom's left leg might now belong to Michael Flatley. Finally the horse's owner runs across to Tom pushing the onlookers out of the way and unplugs the horse. Gala comes to a sudden stop. Tom gets up and takes the applause from the onlookers as the Keoghs are asked to leave the arcade.

i wish i was in dixie

AOIFE NÍ OISTÍN

The day crawls grey and blurry into my brain as I push the sleeping mask from my eyes. For a moment I'm not even aware of what has woken me. I check the clock. Half-past one. Then the insidiously merry sound breaches my earplugs and launches its attack. Awoken again by my Nemesis, another day's sleep disturbed. The natural enemy of the night-shift worker is the cheerful ice-cream man and his chirpy ice-cream van.

Sunny days like this he must feel himself

King of the World, or at least of a small section of Bray. Everyone smiles to hear him coming. Little children rush toward him with bright faces, loose change jangling in their pockets. He is holidays and sand and raspberry sauce. He is shorts and sandals and chocolate flake. He is the sound of summer and the whole world loves him. Little does he suspect the resentment and loathing that oozes out between the slats of the venetian blinds in No. 24. He has no idea that, far from smiling, I curse and seethe with frustrated sleep when he and his noisemobile turn down my street. Never will he guess the hideous tortures I have devised for him. He doesn't know yet that an innocent ice-cream cone can be an instrument of pain.

Some days I dream of running, still pyjamaed, out into the street, the sleeping mask perched on my forehead, and, like a deranged Lone Ranger, shouting at the happy faces and the gorging children to please BE QUIET! A brief stunned silence as I march back to bed, followed by the shrill wail of the fattest child of all as his ice-cream drops in a soft splat by the side of the road.

It used to be the old *Match of the Day* theme tune he played, then 'The Yellow Rose of Texas'. Once I could have sworn I heard Brahm's 'Lullaby', but surely not even he could be so cruel? Day after day, broken sleep after broken sleep, his latest jangling nightmare winds itself into my beleaguered brain: 'I wish I was in Dixie'. I wish one of us was in Dixie and if I ever get my hands on him he'll wish it too.

Pulling the sleeping mask down over my eyes, I turn over and plot as I wait for silence and sleep. I'm saving to buy myself an ice-cream van. We'll soon see how well everyone loves the sleep-splitting sound of summer as I drive around the estates of Bray at half-past one in the morning, blaring the *Lone Ranger* theme music and looking for the ice-cream man's house.

the pleasure dog

DECLAN MACHUGH

I used to see him quite regularly. Perhaps
three or four times a week. He was never up
early in the morning so it was mostly on my
way home from work. He'd usually be
found in the same area, at the entrance to
the estate in which I lived.

Sometimes he'd be sprawled out in the
middle of the road like a starfish, seemingly
fast asleep. He never moved so I used to have
to steer the car around him. Often I'd toot
the horn, more by way of saying hello, but

he never even lifted his head out of curiosity. Other times he'd be sitting on the pavement proudly like the Sphinx.

I'd see him on his travels too. Where he was going and why was anyone's guess. It wasn't where he was going that amused me but the way in which he went. He had a loping, carefree gait unlike any other dog I had ever seen. Every time I saw him he never failed to bring a smile to my face. That's why I named him 'The Pleasure Dog'.

He was speckled brown and white in colour and had a shapely, intelligent-looking head. He oozed a quiet kind of confidence and went about his business in a very dignified, unhurried manner. The other dogs in the estate used to chase cars quite regularly but not him. He just didn't seem bothered by all of that.

One thing that always made me laugh was the way he used to sit, paws on the road with his behind on the footpath. It was as if his front paws were too long and he had to sit that way. I remember deciding that any dog that I would ever have in the future would be trained to sit in that way too.

One evening I was out for a walk when we happened upon each other. I smiled to myself as I had hoped to bump into him. I stopped as he came close and I put out my hand. I had never petted him before and was unsure if it was to be allowed. He let me scratch his ear and snuggled into my leg. And there we stood, me scratching his head and pulling his floppy ears and he, well, just letting me do it. And then he was gone, not stopping to look back.

We never met again. I moved out soon after but often think about my old friend. He still makes me smile.

one august morning

CIARA CONSIDINE

Free at last and I feel like I'm flying. The morning is crystal clear as I weave through traffic on my slinky racer. It's been over a year and I have missed this bike. Motherhood, though welcome, has brought much change, and I miss the ability to rush out the door at a moment's notice. But right now, whizzing down the North Circular Road, it's as though I'm emerging anew. Baby is safe in her daddy's arms, and I'm on a mission.

Today we're going to a wedding – our

first day away from three-month-old Romy
– and I'm in town early to exchange a
garment. A quick visit to Arnotts and then
it's the organisational mayhem involved in
getting baby to her grandparents. But so far
I'm making good time. The glittering
morning tells me to have faith.

This old racer is my favourite bike,
though it's not technically mine, it's my husband's. He's had it forever. It's a bit battered,
but there's grace in the old girl. It's the only
bike I've ridden regularly that hasn't been
stolen, and for that reason alone, it's close to
my heart.

I've just reached my destination when it
hits me, a hollow thud. I've left behind the
lock. There's no time to return. I must find
a solution. An innocent trip has suddenly
become a battle between myself and the
menacing elements of city life. If I am
defeated, I will have lost the morning and all
its promise. I remember a friend's advice,
and ask the universe to help me out.

On Abbey Street the sunshine bounces
off the pavement. A lone coffee drinker sits
at Arnotts' street-side café, almost invisible in
the bright light. In an instant I see that the
universe has delivered. He has been chosen
to mind my bike! I approach and ask: 'Are
you going to be here for a few minutes?'

And then I see it. The bleary eyes, the limp posture. At first I'm not sure if he's drunk or stoned, but it's clear he's in a bad way. I have approached him, and now I want to flee. With unexpected clarity, he seizes on my dilemma: 'Dew you want me to mind your bike?' The words come out in a slur.

My urge to run does battle with my urge to have faith and, as our gazes lock, we silently acknowledge the small stake of this exchange. Then, before I can think any more, he has taken the bike and I am racing through Arnotts. But it's fifteen minutes before I'm sorted and by now I'm panicking. How will I explain this to my husband? The bike he has lovingly nurtured since childhood has been stolen, because I left it with a drunk on Abbey Street. It seemed like a good idea at the time, I hear myself offering weakly.

I race back through the shop. And there, hovering at the door, expectant-looking, is the kind man – the drunk, the junkie, who knows? – the kind man who has saved my morning. I push a fiver into his hand and hastily thank him. His red eyes sparkle.

'You never know the ones you can trust,' he says. 'Indeed you don't,' I reply, and cycle off into the morning sun. I begin the ascent home, smiling, renewed.

cusack's last stand

SEAN O'CALLAGHAN

Had I been travelling through an airport that day I would have been arrested. The contraband I was carrying would not have passed any of the usual security checks: a junior hacksaw, a small hammer, a multi-functional spanner and two screwdrivers, a Phillips and a flathead, just in case. My body warmer was an ideal garment for carrying the tools I needed to complete my mission.

My passport, in the form of an upper-deck Cusack Stand ticket, was wedged firmly into the breast pocket of my shirt. It was Sunday, 19 September 1993, and Cork and Derry were to do battle in Croke Park for the Sam Maguire. This was to be the last match played in Croker as we knew it back then. Demolition of the Cusack Stand would start the following day.

This wondrous structure where, as a young boy growing up in Cabra West, I had spent countless Sundays with my father as he admitted teams and mentors through 'his gate' at the Hill 16 end of the Cusack Stand. I had met many of the greats of hurling and football as I assisted him in his duties at this hallowed spot. I graduated to selling official souvenir programmes of the many games that graced this great stadium during my early years. As I grew to manhood I was engaged as a stilesman and regularly worked on the stiles that gave access to the structure that was soon to be no more.

On this particular day, I intended to provide myself with a unique souvenir of the place that had played such a big part in my life. Approaching the stiles that lead to the upper deck I indicated to my old stilesman colleague that I wished to hold on to my full ticket as a memento of the game. He let me climb over the stile. He then presented me with a certificate verifying my attendance at

Croker on this special occasion. Intact ticket, certificate, match programme, what more could a fan hope for?

I made my way to section M seat 00071. I unloaded my pockets and set to work. The spanner and the screwdrivers were no match for the years of rust and several coats of paint that attached themselves to the section of seating I was trying to dismantle. My only hope was the junior hacksaw. I set about cutting the back section of the seat bearing the number that corresponded to the intact ticket, amid howls of laughter from adjacent fans. The Garda on duty chuckled and blithely ignored my attempts at demolition as I told him I was only making it easier for the lads starting work tomorrow.

Soon my mission was complete. I now had a most unique collection of souvenirs of the day and place. The ticket, certificate, seat back and programme are now all framed in red and white (Cork and Derry colours) and enjoy a permanent resting place on a wall at home.

nits

WINIFRED POWER

I hate it when Mum does my nits.

I brought a nit note home from school.
I read it to Mum from the back of the car.

'*We are sorry to inform you that there has been an outb …*'

'OUTBreak,' said Mum.

'*… of head lice in the school,*' I read. '*This is a comm …*'

'COMMunity,' said Mum.

'*… problem and we ask parents to do follow these simple inst …*'

'*INSTructions,*' said Mum.

'*below.*'

That meant another fight. I kick and scream and Mum shouts and tells me if I don't stop moving she is going to cut my hair short. It *hurts* when she combs my hair. She uses a small metal comb and *drags* it through my hair. She puts conditioner through it to make it easier she says. She says I'm lucky I'm not in pain all the time, and this will prepare me for when I am an adult – it will make me stronger.

It's not fair. I get nits all the time. Mum says I go to school nit-free and come home *crawling with them.* She says they're having parties on my head and that they are learning their spellings with me. We think my nits can read.

She says could I be a spy and find out if my friends at school's parents do their nits.

'No,' I shouted, 'I won't.'

'But you could be a detective,' she says. 'Wouldn't you like that? You just watch out for who is scratching, and then ask them if their mum or dad do their nits.'

'I won't spy on my friends,' I say.

Mum's friend Anne is a nurse, and Mum got her to explain to me exactly how the nits work. Anne said nits can have baby nits every seven hours. So if I have five nits at four o'clock, I could have twenty-five by the time I go to bed and even more when I wake up in the morning. Nits just grow and grow.

Mum hates the nits. She shouts at them and gives out to them when she's combing my hair. She says it's hard on her because she's a *vegetarian* and it's not really in her to kill living things. (What about carrots? I don't ask.)

Mum gives out because she has to check *all* our heads, and she says it's hard because she's a *single parent*, so there's nobody to check her head. Then she's worried her friends will get them too, so she tells them to check *their* hair. Then everybody goes *Ugh* and starts scratching, and Mum goes red.

When Conor and I went on holidays to Granny's, Mum spent ages telling Granny how to check my hair, and how she would pack my special nit comb, and could Granny please check me *every day*. When we come back from Granny's, Mum checks my hair. I am fine.

But Mum has forgotten to ask Granny to check Conor – he is crawling with them.

coming home

MARY HAYWARD

It was raining as I made my way, chilled to
the bone, from the departure gate to the
plane. The air stewards rattled trolleys up and
down the aisle, attentive to all, serving
brandy, whiskey, beer and soft drinks in soft
voices. The engines droned; businessmen
rattled copies of the *Examiner*, napped and
stretched. How many times, I wondered, had
she made the trip across the Irish Sea during
her short years. Blinding flashes of her
startled me, her hitching up her skirt

teaching me to dance, giving me tips on how to pull guys, caking my face with make-up and blow-drying my hair, giggling all the while. Her prancing down the avenue, the Ulster Schools' Netball Cup held aloft, bowing extravagantly to one and all. She was a poppy dancing in a summer meadow. Now in stilled silence she rested alongside primroses and awakening catkins, under the shadow of derelict cotton mills and a million miles from Derry.

We landed with a bump and disembarked into a crisp, clear afternoon. I was first through the arrivals gate and was assaulted by two very excited small boys. I buried my face in freckles and curls, hugs and kisses. The baby smelling of milk and sleep cooed, chubby arms outstretched. Hubby didn't get a look in. Everyone was talking at once, shouting each other down.

The road home was lit with daffodils and the sea glittered. Stopping at Greystones to give the boys a treat, they skimmed stones, flung monstrous ribbons of seaweed at each other and watched fishermen load up their boats with lobsterpots. Then off to Greta's Garden Centre for bright-blue forget-me-nots, the colour of her eyes, to plant in the dark mossy area at the back of the garden, a memento of our growing.

memories of another life

EDDIE NAUGHTON

It was 1964, my seventeenth year, and I remember my father standing in the steamy bathroom of our house, stripped to the waist, his heavy braces hanging like thick leather thongs by his side. I remember the open razor still poised in his hand, his half-shaved face a mask of disbelief.

'Ballymena!' he cried, incredulous.

'Yes,' I said. 'Train's leaving at half ten.'

'But you never said a thing about this!'

It was true I hadn't told anyone about

my plans. But that was because I was vague and unsure about what I was doing and where I was going at that time in my life. And besides, I was beyond persuasion that anybody cared what I did or where I went.

I had filled out the coupon in my father's newspaper some weeks before just to see what would happen. Then to my surprise and delight I received a train ticket to travel and undergo what turned out to be nothing more than a cursory medical examination. Three weeks after that I received another ticket, this time one-way. It was make-your-mind-up time for me. What had started out as a light-hearted exercise ended up with me spending a few dark hours wrestling with my thoughts before deciding that I would go. There was really nothing at home to hold me. I was unemployed and had been turned down yet again for a job the day before my second ticket to travel arrived.

Having made my decision I felt a strange elation. Not for what lay ahead but for what I was leaving behind: constant rows and arguments, familial storms over hitherto un-contested certainties. I was anxious now to embark on my new life. I wanted to be away.

In the bathroom, I looked at my father and shrugged. Then I moved towards the hall door. Under my arm I had a brown-paper parcel, which was tied up with a string of yellow wool. As I got to the door my father called after me.

'Wait, Edward!'

He fished in his pocket and came up with some money that he pressed into my hand.

'Here,' he said. 'You might be able to use this.'

Then he began to cry. I looked at him, indifferent. At that time I had no concept of tears other than those caused by physical pain. I pocketed the money and mumbled a thank you. Then I opened the hall door and stepped out. My father stood there speechless and pathetic, a tear running down the unshaven side of his face like a rivulet through snow. I turned away from him and walked down the passage and out the gate without looking back.

Later that day I became a British soldier.

twenty-first century romance

ANNE WATERSON

Is romance alive today? For me, the whole process of falling in love has been severely tarnished by the introduction of that small metal box that accompanies us everywhere we go.

I met Jamie three years ago and over these three years 90 per cent of our conversations have been conducted through those small, irritating, regular intruders into our lives – the mobile phone. We met when we were both students working in a call centre in the west of Ireland. We started out well as friends who had a good laugh together but at the end of the summer, when we returned to college, our blossoming relationship was suddenly infiltrated by 'the Mobile'.

'The Mobile' had now entered the equation and our cosy twosome had become a slightly overcrowded foursome. His mobile and mine got on very well together; the text conversations could carry on for hours and became quite intimate, far more so than Jamie and I had ever managed on our own! This was fine, until after a while things began to get serious.

Mobile phones are cleverly designed – before, if something was difficult to say you had to gather your courage, put your heart in their hands and just speak. 'The Mobile' has removed this particular form of terror – if it's too hard to say, just text it. There's no fear of stumbling over words, blushing crimson or having to look at the object of your desire and, cringing, wait for their response. It's so much easier to let your thumb do the work and reduce what could be one of the most enchanting moments of your life to a few crudely shortened words on a small flashing screen.

So when Jamie told me one day that he loved me, I waited expectantly for the euphoria, the light-headedness, the sheer ecstasy of the moment. Then, after a few seconds I realised that Jamie wasn't saying those magical words but rather it was this small metal thing sitting in the palm of my hand, and I was on my own! Surely it wasn't meant to be like this?

Three years on I'm still waiting to actually hear Jamie say those words to me, although I admit I was happy even just to see them on the little screen. But has romance in the twenty-first century really come to this? Won't somebody please prove me wrong? Oh, wait, I hear it beeping on my desk. It's probably Jamie, I should probably text him back, it's what we do after all.

the graveyard

Linda Richardson

Tramore graveyard can be beautiful. The old granite church in the background, the salty sea air, the watery blue of a winter sky, the birds always squawking overhead.

The big solid block that I stand at represents a young man, my brother, my little boy's uncle. A strong young man who was bursting with life. A freckled smiler. A demon on the football pitch, a bright young fellow who always got his exams without too much studying. So many friends, such lovely girlfriends, always landing sunny-side up in any situation. Well, almost always. Life over at the age of twenty-three. So many other graves in Ireland, full with strong, healthy young men. Men who lived life to bursting point, then left, way too soon.

Eoin, my little son, stands solemnly before the headstone in beautiful, unconscious mimicry of others he has seen standing silently at prayer. His head of little golden curls is bowed and his hands are held together. I stand beside him, and realise that I too am unconsciously mimicking someone at prayer, for I gave up prayer and all its trappings a long time ago. While I love the peace that this place brings and the ritual of ceremonies that helped us through the first days, and the kindness of the priests, a religious upbringing is not one which I am passing on to my son. Eoin's only connection to the church are these visits to uncle Keith's 'special place', as we call it.

Eoin has drifted away, running around the tombstones and finding puddles to jump in and splash. He stops and gazes entranced at the workmen at the back of the graveyard. They are erecting Tramore's new millennium cross.

It's getting cold, time to return to granny's house. Eoin chatters on about his new Montessori teacher and everything he is learning. He runs to his granny's lap.

'Well, what did you see on your walk today, Eoin?'

'Oh, it's beautiful, Granny. In Keith's special place they are making new statues.'

'Really, what kind of statues?'

'They are beautiful, there's a big new one, reaching right into the sky.'

'What's that?'

'It's a big, big, big statue of a plus sign.'

I look at my mother to check she hasn't been insulted. She snuggles him tightly and we laugh and cry though our broken hearts.

shiny things

AILISH CONNELLY

I like the spire. Maybe I even love the spire. Because several good things happened the day the spire got his hat on, got its final piece into place and finally glittered down on Dublin. On all the thousands who turned out to cheer and scorn, to howl in derision or simply to be there. Something to tell the grandkids. A small gem to remember for yourself, of a wet Wednesday.

Me, I had a scan appointment to get to. My youngest child was in utero, a full twenty weeks old, and the Rotunda beckoned. So in we went, myself and himself, him gleeful and giddy, delighted, being the big daddy and all. Me quietly praying everything was well, bladder bursting. They can't read the scan unless one's bladder is bursting.

'Hop up,' says the nurse, and I do. She smears on the cold gel and the monitor sparks to life. 'There's the heart,' she points, 'and the head, the spine and the legs.'

'Is everything all right?' says I.

'Is it a boy?' says he.

The nurse ignores him.

'Everything is just fine.'

'But is it a boy?' he demands. 'Are there any dangly bits?'

'I can't see,' she smiles patiently. She gets these nutters in daily, her eyes explain.

'Well, can't you turn it round so,' says himself. Matter of factly. 'So that you can get a good look.'

We both ignore him.

'Loo?' I ask desperately.

'I'll show you,' she nods. 'You can search the screen for dangly bits while we are gone,' she offers. He is now practically on top of the monitor such is his eagerness. One princess is enough, he has declared. He is serious.

As we leave the hospital I remind him of

something we talked about several times before. The ring.

'You promised,' says I.

'I did,' he agrees.

Ten years, third baby on the way, it's not too much to ask. I feel lucky today. We round the top of O'Connell St. It's quiet, no traffic. A crowd has gathered, expectation in the air.

'Let's go choose the ring and be back in time for the top going on,' says he. We choose it, a simple platinum solitaire. Not so big it would blind you, not so small you'd have to squint.

Now I'm here again. In the new plaza, in O'Connell Street, pushing the buggy. We turn into the warm September sun, stretch out our arms and feel the diamond glint of the spire on our skin, my sixteen-month-old toddler and I. And he laughs and squeals, we hold hands, his soft sticky one folded into mine, and I close my eyes, silently fingering the platinum band, then the smooth surface of the stone, feeling the heat of the day on my upturned face, remembering another day.

real life

JOSEPH SWEENEY

Garda Ryan here. Ex-Garda Ryan now. My last day on the job was five months ago. Got a call about a woman who had collapsed in Grafton Street. I found her under a bundle of clothes. African. She was having a baby. I recall it clearly still.

I arrive, survey the situation, pretending to be calm. It is unreal – my last day and I get *this*. The deepest part of me wants to turn tail. I feel my stomach churn. I amn't trained for this.

I loosen her clothes. I can't believe I'm doing this. They are so tight that no baby, no matter how pushy, could get out into this world. People just walk on. The African woman contracts, breathes, her face contorts and, totally silent up to now, she suddenly lets out an ear-splitting scream. Jessye Norman volume. That gets attention. That stops people up.

'How can we help?' mute eyes seem to say. They look as if they can hardly help themselves. They can't help staring anyway. It's better than any soap. Better than reality TV. This is reality.

A baby arrives to a large, ashamed audience. A soggy little thing sliding out on a river of blood and waters. Life renewing itself. What is it? Boy or girl? Will it be an Irish citizen? Or illegal African? Who cares about that right now? She's beautifully ugly.

An ambulance arrives and takes the huge woman in the flowing, coloured clothes away, holding the dark wrinkly baby. She has not even noticed me. 'You're welcome, Ma'am,' I say to the departing ambulance.

But something inside me had been quietly overwhelmed. My last day on the job and I find something just beginning, for the very first time. I feel strangely emotional, light-headed. Something profound has caught me off-balance. I'm no longer a guard, seeing life in terms of rules, as legal or illegal. Life is greater than the sum of its parts. While we worry life moves. While we argue and legislate and enforce, it moves still. Screaming and in pain.

People look after the ambulance and wonder. The strange shock is gone. The extraordinary event is over. People don't know what has occurred, and vaguely wonder before passing on, Did anytning really happen?

'Just a vagrant being moved on,' someone mutters. 'We heard about them on the news,' says another. 'They come here to have their baby. To get Irish citizenship.'

'Maybe,' a child whispers to her mother, 'maybe she didn't really have a baby.' Was it a trick? A clever trick to beat the system. Maybe she had it hidden under her clothes all along. The thing is already losing itself in rumour, suspicion, myth.

I'm beyond this now. I've retired. Moved on. I'm looking for a bigger world. Like that African woman and her baby, I need a new beginning. After thirty-five years I'm still looking for my life. Real life.

the new house

LETIZIA ARESU

So here I finally am. I've collected the keys
and for the first time I can spend time alone
in my new house. The existence of the
previous owner is barely recorded by the
expensive male fragrance that still fills the
master bedroom.

'You must be so happy now that you've
got your own place. You'll even be in for
Christmas!' Yes, technically speaking I'll
have moved in but for Christmas I am going
home to Italy, a habit I picked up from ten

years of renting in Dublin, Paris, Stuttgart, Antwerp and finally Cork. 'No wonder you can't put down roots. When you get your own place you'll settle.' That's what I have been hearing for the last four years whenever I said that I didn't fit in here, I didn't belong. 'Anyway, if you hadn't told me you were only renting I could never have guessed that you were just a tenant.' Gee thanks. To me home was always made by my pictures, books and all that stuff I have accumulated over the years. Following me around Europe move after move, gathering dust and stains from all over, every bit of furniture acquired a history, memories and a bit of myself. The four walls around my home never meant much to me; every place I lived in was my own for the length of time I spent in it. When I arrived in Ireland owning those four walls became an obsession. 'Rent is money down the drain.' Well, it depends on what you want from life.

I walk around the upstairs of my new house. 'Four-bedroom detached and with a Jacuzzi bath, I bet you feel settled now!' That word again. Besides the faint perfume in the air there are no traces of soul; the paint is spotless, no mould on the bathroom tiles, not a single forgotten item. I slowly make my way downstairs. The place looks equally perfect: shiny wooden floors, kitchen with an island, separate dining-room and a big garden. I'll finally be able to join in all those conversations I felt excluded from until now, the only kind of conversation available: 'No holidays this year – we're starting on the extension, the attic conversion is next … I'm shopping around for conservatories …' It's as though the people around me didn't have lives, they had houses instead.

I sit on the bottom stair and look straight into the sitting-room, imagining my book-shelves and Moroccan rug there, picturing my teak table and chairs with the coconut mat underneath in the dining-room and the Turkish mirror on the wall that my best friend gave me as a house-warming gift. I wonder what impact they'll have on the next buyer. Pity I had to go all the way, but now that I am finally owner of my not-so-little square of land I am sure that I didn't want a house after all, I wanted a life.

what do you know?

MAGS TREANOR

When I was a teenager back in the eighties, a school friend told me not to link her arm.

'They'll think we're "lezzers",' she said. I'd never heard the word before so she enlightened me to this sexual abnormality suffered by a disgraceful minority. It sounded bad enough to be up there with afflictions such as leprosy and on a moral par with large-scale drug dealing. I reckoned my best bet was to stick with the other species, the ones from Mars: men.

Along came the nineties. The wild years

of being out of the clutches of parents and not yet immersed in the restraints of marriage. And there was travel. Different countries, different cultures. London, Munich, Amsterdam. It was quite shocking to see same-sex partners walk hand in hand or arm in arm along large boulevards or in giant art galleries. Now I was forced to question the validity of what I had learned at home. But it wasn't home, and I felt almost embarrassed at the thought of any of them doing that in my country.

Once though, at a party in Dublin, I saw two women kissing. I was transfixed. Part of me horrified but also amused at my own ignorance. I myself got married, had children and lived a comfortable suburban life. But that too wasn't as simple a solution to life as had originally been painted. It wasn't long until our differences became so irreconcilable that we parted ways.

By now it was the next century, so I decided not to look as far as Mars, or even mainland Europe. I met her in Dublin and she was drop-dead gorgeous. For once in my life I could have hugged the Celtic Tiger for its lack of taxis. She lived nearby. I could come back for a cup of tea, and in an hour it would be quieter and we could book a taxi by phone. We did all that, but not until late into the next day. The cup of tea, as promised, was served in bed, with toast and marmalade on a groovy-looking tray with a marigold from her garden.

'Funny,' she said, plonking herself on the side of the bed, gorgeous in a crimson morning robe. 'To be so intimate and not even know if you take milk or sugar.'

'Just milk,' I replied, sitting up in bed, and all of a sudden I knew that this 'not knowing' *was* the intimacy.

i will never find love

ORLA MARTIN

Leaning on a Zanussi in Power City, I realise I will never find love.

'Get your fella to plumb in the machine.' The assistant squints at me in his red jumper when I ask about the washing machine on sale at €299.

'But I'm on my own. Can't I get a plumber?'

'You can rig this up yourself,' he says. 'Piping underneath the sink. Sure why would you need a plumber. Any fool can plumb a washing machine.'

Off he trundles, leaving a faint whiff of cardboard, towards a wall of Sony wide-screen TVs. All shining bright.

'But I don't know anything about plumbing,' I say to a nearby microwave (10 per cent off this week only). 'How will I ever find love?'

'It's the water pressure,' the voice from under the sink calls.

'Sorry?' I am not going to cry, having waited two weeks for my handsome plumber to arrive in his blue van to lift my washing machine from the depths of its styrofoam prison.

'You'll have to contact the Corporation. I've never seen pressure this bad. Have you actually bought this place?' Still from under the sink the voice leaks.

'Yes.' I will not cry. 'Is there nothing you can do?'

'Flats. No planning for this kind of thing. No workmanship at all. Just don't leave the house when you turn the washing machine on. Keep an eye on it or the place will flood.'

'Right.' Tears are welling. 'Would you like a cup of tea?'

'No, thanks,' says the plumber. 'That'll be €70. Could your fella not have done this job?'

'I don't have a bloody fella!'

canvassing

MICHAEL McLOUGHLIN

I blame Richie Ryan. I was ten, standing in a concrete school yard in his constituency, on a local election day in the 1970s. It was deserted, but for me. The school was closed, turned into a citadel of democracy. In the middle of the afternoon, in swept the Minister's Mercedes. Out he hopped. Seeing no one else, he came over, shook my hand and talked. The news junkie of third class was hooked.

Thirty years later, it was my turn. Well,

not quite. But after years of dithering, I put my name in the ring for the local elections. I was selected to fight a bear pit of a constituency. The twenty-first-century tools available to a candidate are very simple – leaflets, friends and shoe leather. Politics in Ireland is the last thing sold door to door, and the wealthier the area, the more the voters want you on their doorstep. As a new candidate, you can't talk about the things you did or didn't do. All you can talk about is what you *will* do differently, ferret out the voters' concerns and talk about them.

So after six thousand houses, and two weeks to go to polling day, I was learning. Not an old hand, but more weather-beaten politically than when I had started.

I was canvassing in my 'heartland' when I came across a neat, tidy house. The door was answered.

'I have been lying in wait for you,' he snarled, 'waiting for you to call.' He spoke with fire and venom. Shocked, I scanned back through my life to see whether there was some unforgivable crime that I had committed. I quickly reviewed the period of my life between first confession and the day that I met the Minister. Since I had met Richie, I had kept my nose clean, generally avoiding acts of murder, violence or robbery. I had a clear conscience. But it was my current lack of policies that were to haunt me.'

'What is your policy,' he said, our noses four inches apart, 'on numbers on gates?' I asked whether I had heard him right. I had. There was only one solution. In a variation of Hoover's promise of a chicken in every pot, I promised a number on every gate, feverishly wondering whether we had one at home. He might check. He was not yet satisfied, and though I retreated backwards down the garden path to the gate, he remained the furious four inches from my face. He eventually calmed down. I stumbled on.

Trying to garner every vote, I went back in the final days, not canvassing but delivering leaflets – one last message exhorting support. I came to the house, paused and thought, maybe I can get in and out quickly without knocking. I went up the drive, pushed the letter box and, just at the point of no return, the door opened. I froze. A middle-aged woman appeared.

'Did you get a rough time here a few weeks ago?' she asked, knowingly. I paused. 'You'll be allright for two No. 1s here,' she said. 'Thanks for calling.'

hard to swallow

ANONYMOUS

I've talked to a few doctors about the effects of Ecstasy. The thing is, they always seem to be enjoying it as much as me. On a recent night in a heaving dance club I got chatting away to a girl like me, in her twenties. She'd swallowed the required dose of pills to bring on the customary jaw-chewing and eye-rolling. Turns out, she's a doctor and was due for a shift in a Dublin hospital two days later. She joked that she'd be the one needing the hospital bed.

Everything seems so simple when you're floating away on these happy pills. Life just seems to untangle itself. Your inability to hold anything back liberates you and brings on some incredible conversations with some incredible people.

Before 'coming up' on the five euro pill, everything is normal. All your insecurities are firmly in place as you secretly envy a dress on another girl with a gorgeous figure. When you're 'up', everything is clear; you feel as if you could conquer the world with love in one night. In fact, you'll more than likely stride over to the girl you noticed earlier and tell her how beautiful you think she is and that you secretly envied her dress. This is done without any fear of her laughing at you, attacking you or assuming you're a lesbian. She's probably 'up' at this point too and will thus be very receptive to your compliments. I remember one night telling a girl I liked her top whereby she dragged me to the ladies' toilets, peeled it off and gave it to me with complete and unadulterated sincerity and kindness.

Of course there are downsides. You learn it in first-year physics at school. For every action there's an equal and opposite reaction. For the rush of happiness to your brain which you experience on that one night, there's at least two days of hell to pay afterwards. During the comedown you can sometimes catch yourself pondering suicide. You have to keep reminding yourself that there's just a lack of that happiness chemical called serotonin in your brain. Every time I hear about a young suicide victim, I can't help wondering what they did the weekend beforehand.

Politicians talk and talk and talk about drugs like Ecstasy. In fact, sometimes they talk so much that I can't help wondering if they've swallowed a pill or two before appearing on *Marian Finucane* or *Prime Time*. The other night out clubbing I befriended the daughter of a politician. Whilst her daddy was busy talking the talk about Ireland's drug problem, she was happily partaking in the crisis.

Watch out, smug middle-Ireland: it's not on your doorstep, it's in your porch.

coffee at eleven

FIONA MARSHALL

I suppose I was always looking for John
Wayne. I wanted a man who would sweep
me off my feet, just like he did to Maureen
O'Hara in the film *The Quiet Man*. Instead I
married the Milky Bar Kid.

I always went to Bewley's in Grafton
Street for my Friday treat. A cup of Bewley's
coffee and a chocolate éclair. And I was
sitting in my usual seat facing the framed
prints of The Four Courts when I first set
eyes on him. And it was far from Maureen

O'Hara that I looked with a blob of cream hanging from my lower lip. But, oh my, he was just like John Wayne as he nodded to me and gently tipped his lower lip. I fumbled for my napkin and wiped my mouth.

Every Friday at one o'clock, I left the dreary solicitor's office I worked in as a secretary and half-walked and half-ran to Bewleys. I always got there before him. After that first sighting I replaced my delicious éclair with an oatmeal cookie. They were easier to eat and besides, everytime I saw him sashay into the restaurant my stomach greeted my mouth.

He was so dapper. Always, always in a suit and tie and never without a silk hand-kerchief in his breast pocket. He read the *Financial Times* and drank so many cups of coffee that I'd lose count. Then one Friday in November he came in and, still shaking the sleet from his hat, he walked straight over to me.

'Matt Dillon,' he said, proffering his hand.

'Rosie,' I stammered.

'I was wondering if you would allow me to take you out to dinner?' he asked. I know I said yes, because before I knew it I'd made arrangements to meet him the following night outside Bewley's at seven-thirty.

I was the eldest. The night I was to meet

Matt, my mother went into labour just as I was about to leave the house. Pandemonium broke out as her labour accelerated so quickly that my poor father couldn't even get her into the car from the kitchen. And that's where my brother was born, screaming his way into the world on the kitchen floor. There was great excitement and panic, so much so that Matt Dillon escaped from my thoughts for almost an hour. It was only after my mother was taken away in the ambulance with my father driving behind her in hot pursuit that reality took over once again.

I ran all the way from York Street to Grafton Street. I was forty minutes late. He was gone and I never saw him again. I still went to Bewley's every Friday and always left with a heavy heart, somehow realising I'd never see him again.

I married my husband ten months later. He was an accountant. 'A good steady job,' my father reassured me on my wedding morning. Not a week went by in my twenty-year marriage that Tom didn't remind me of that fact. Especially when he was kicking my head as I lay on the kitchen floor. Or whatever floor I lay curled up on in the house, where I tried to bring up our children and shield them from the nightmare that was my life. My life was like a Picasso painting. All sharp angles, nothing ever flowing freely or easily like, say, a Monet, where everything seemed calm and fluid.

Most Fridays I went into Bewley's and sat in that same seat, sometimes with a baby in my womb or on my lap or sitting opposite me. Sometimes when the four of them grew up and the boxes and boots had diminished I allowed myself wonder, if only my brother hadn't been born that night … If only Tom had never walked into the office where I worked. If only Matt had waited for longer. So many 'if onlys'.

valentine record

MARY COOKE

Tonight is Valentine's night and my highlight will be shopping in Tesco's – nice and quiet after six. I presume it will be quieter than usual.

I might buy the Tesco's meal for two and keep the second dish for Sunday, but I expect there probably will be a rush on for those couples who've forgotten or can't get a table for two in an overcrowded restaurant.

Valentine's Day is similar to magazine reading. There is greater joy in the anticipation of the purchase than the actual read itself on your cream-coloured couch. It's the same with Valentine's Day.

I look back on Valentines past. When you are in a relationship the day borders on insignificance with a jaded sarcasm at the lesser mortals who fall for the razzmatazz. After the first few years both you and your partner agree over morning coffee not to be seduced by the heavy-handed play of marketing, not by the choked carnations in the corner of the local shop or the over-priced Valentine's dinner menu displayed in the little Italian down the road. The stories on the radio or the ads on TV can all be dismissed as something for the foolish and the misled. In reality most women as they clear the cups afterwards want some Valentine token, a recognition that they are somebody's Valentine, something they can acknowledge over the water port in the office the next day.

However, Valentine's Day when single is a big deal. Full stop.

'What will you be doing?' I am asked, almost a Christmas-Day poised question. A novice single worries; a veteran single plans, invites her single friends around or has a bath with mineral salts (what would a single woman do without a bath). The key to survival is group survival – just watch *Sex and the City* for that.

The reality is that I am happy, sitting here with my onion bhajis, incense burning, watching a Channel 4 reality TV show on bigamy. This is twenty-first-century living: you want what you haven't got, then you get it and realise it is not all it is cracked up to be. Maybe I am just cynical. There is more in anticipation.

suspicion

TIM CRONIN

The other girl stood motionless as the water lapped around her waist. Her eyes, full of envy, were fixed on us as we splashed and played without a care. She approached us cautiously and enquired, 'Are you her daddy?'

'Yes – this is Emma. She is just two. What's your name?'

'Sinead.' Then she immediately blurted out, 'You know I don't have a daddy!'

A wave of sympathy came over me. I thought, 'You poor child, of course you have a daddy. Maybe he is dead, absconded, thrown out or perhaps unknown? But you must have a daddy.' I dared not ask for fear of upsetting her.

My legs were outstretched on the floor of the toddler pool as I sat relaxing in the warm water. Suddenly and unexpectedly she grabbed me by both ankles and proceeded to drag me helplessly around in a circle. I felt I should shout, 'Please don't do that! What will everyone think?' The lifeguard is looking. Those people are wondering what's going on. No! I'm afraid it's not on. It's not on for a man to be playing like this with a strange child.

I'd love to play, to fool, to horse about, act as surrogate daddy for a brief moment. But it cannot be, not with all the scandals and revelations that have arisen. Even the most innocent actions can easily be misconstrued.

I managed to free myself from her grasp and gain a footing on the tiled floor. Some swim-floats were nearby so I grabbed one and flung it to the far end of the pool in the hope that it would serve to distract her attention. She waded to retrieve it and turned towards me to see what the next bit of fun would be. But sensing that I wasn't willing to participate further in her games she moved dejectedly to the side and sat on the edge with her legs dangling in the water.

There was a sharp tapping from the viewing gallery window. A middle-aged woman mouthed a muffled instruction while pointing to the exit. Sinead rose obediently and moved with urgency towards the changing rooms. She turned into the bare block corridor and was gone.

the things you believe

AOIFE DUGGAN

When I was a child, I believed everything adults told me. I had blind and unquestioning faith in my parents and siblings and took them at their word. I believed my sister when she told me that Chipsticks were addictive and warily steered clear of them in the shops, running away from anyone who innocently offered me a Chipstick in the school playground ... those pushers, I would not succumb. I'd seen people go to three packets a day and I didn't have the pocket money to sustain that kind of habit and, before you know it, I would have been raiding the copper box on the mantelpiece for the 8p to buy bags in secret – that was one slippery slope that I was not prepared to slide down.

I believed my mother when she told me that ladies don't fart, which made me question my gender at a ridiculously early age because I was certainly capable of the action and if I wasn't a lady, then what the hell was I?

For several months in fourth class, I believed that I was going to do something really terrible and end up in jail for the rest of my life and I would never see my family and I knew I wasn't tough enough to survive the rigors of prison life and that it would be the end of me. I lost at least three weeks of sleep over it.

I believed that I was going to be a professional disco dancer when I grew up. I practised my craft in the sitting-room on sunny Sundays to the melodic strains of Abba, when I believed that I had the house to myself. I was on fire, I was the music, I was at one with Bjorn, Benny, Frida and Agnetha. I was the laughing stock of the household as my family observed my antics through the net curtains.

I believed that if I stayed quiet and still for long enough I would become invisible. I practised this for hours under beds and tables and in the toy press, refusing to answer when called, and emerging when least expected.

I believed that if I sat by the trees at the side of our house without moving a muscle and keeping my arm outstretched a robin would land on my arm and we would become friends.

I believed that when I slept, my toys came to life. I believed that my family was the epicentre of the universe and that all things started and ended in our little house. I believed that God was with me all day every day. I believed that Dan Murphy would kill us with a pitchfork and bury us in his sheds if he caught us climbing the trees in his fields one more time. I believed that my mother and the pope were infallible. I believed that dandelions were fairies and that if you let a woodlouse crawl all over you you would get a new dress (I actively sought these critters out as I was always getting cast-offs which swam on me. It never happened but I still believed each and every time).

I believed that when I left the confessional box, after unburdening my weighty sins, I was pure and clean and without stain. I would run from the church, down the hill, all the way home, delighted that the whole ordeal was over for another six weeks. I rarely made it the whole way without having some impure thought which ruined everything and had to go on the list for my next confession. So once I started, there was no point in stopping and before the day would be out, I would be up to my armpits in impure thoughts – better to get them out of the way and try to be good tomorrow.

I believed that everything I ever wanted was in my home town. I believed that Mick Fitzmaurice would eventually realise that, despite the twenty-year age gap, he would have to marry me because deep down he thought I was exquisite and he was ferociously in love with me.

I believed that I was going to be famous. I believed that I would see all our dogs again in heaven and that the kittens really did go to 'a farm'. I believed that one day I was going to meet Apollo from *Battlestar Galactica* and live happily ever after in a galaxy far far away (leaving Mick Fitzmaurice broken hearted of course – I wasn't cruel, but Apollo was a captain of a substantial fleet, and Mick Fitz was only a farmer).

I believed that I had been alive before

and used to frequently cite experiences from 'when I was a big girl', which really annoyed my sister. I believed in magic and time travel and Catweazle.

I miss these things more than I care to believe.

a run-in with st brigid

JANE O'ROURKE

I had a run-in with St Brigid. I never had anything against her. In fact, as saints go she must be among the hippest, with echoes of a pagan origin, a nod to Christianity, a few legendary good deeds and an Irish accent. There was a nun at school who kept us enthralled for a whole year with the lives of the saints, but Bríd was the one that stuck in my mind; she was the one with the magic cloak that stretched and stretched to make the plains of the Curragh in Kildare. I often think of her as I pass through on the train, a rolling cloak of yellow gorse and horses. We learned to make St Brigid's Crosses at school too; the classroom floor was covered in rushes as we ran home to give them as presents to our mammies and grannies.

But that was years back, and I, like a lot of my generation, have not so much turned my back on the Church, as side-stepped quietly away. The bookshelves of my friends contain yoga manuals and self-help books now. We are more aware of the coming of Ramadan than Lent. I'm not old enough to remember strict adherence to fish on Fridays, but that would be no sacrifice now. We could have tuna on rye, wholemeal, bagel, Ryvita, nurturing brain cells, sperm count and keeping our hearts happy with lots of Essential Fatty Acids.

But sometimes it's nice to remember, which is why I happily accepted a St Brigid's Cross from my mother. I would hang it in my house as a nice, subtle, eco-friendly reminder of my beginnings. I read the attached card with interest, how the cross was said to protect the home from harm. 'Great,' I thought. 'Between that and the smoke alarm I'll be grand.'

I hooped a piece of thread through the cross and stood on the arm of the couch to hang it on the wall. Then I reached my stockinged foot behind me to step down onto the seat.

I missed and my foot was stepping on air, followed by the rest of me, falling, slowly, backwards. I knew where the coffee table was and I knew my head was going to hit it. I flapped my arms wildly, swimming through the air, trying to make contact with anything that would break my fall.

After several very slow seconds, my elbow crashed onto the coffee table, hero-ically (and suddenly) bearing my eleven stone and saving my head in the process. So when I say I had a run-in with St Brigid, you know now what I mean.

But you know, as much as times have changed, and we in Ireland are evolving into something new, when I lay, curled in a ball on the ground after my fall, rattled and relieved, it was my mother's battle-cry in times of trouble that came to my lips:

'O Jesus … O Jesus, Mary and Joseph … O Jesus.'

how the world works

JOE PHELAN

Twenty years in the Irish Public Service
have convinced me that there is a God.
Once you have seen from the inside how a
country is administered, and realise that
countries with Weapons of Mass Destruct-
ion work the same way, there is no possible
explanation for continued human existence
other than a caring Higher Power.

In a Tom Clancy thriller, senior officials
advise a government which combines decis-
iveness with compassion. The virus is stopped,
the atomic warhead recovered, economic

progress assured, the world saved. That group of senior officials is always well-informed, dedicated, alert. How totally unlike this bunch around the table with me right now!

I suppose they're senior enough all right. Nobody here under forty-five or on less than eighty grand a year. But minutes into this meeting of the Advisory Sub-Committee it became clear that half of them haven't read any briefing papers other than what they wrote themselves. Most of us are only here because our bosses insisted.

I'm working on my favourite doodle. It's a small flower with thousands of petals. The voices drone on ...

'Option three would be a runner if conditions outlined in section F applied ...'

'Management Services feels the optimal way to approach this, going forward, would be as recommended by the Working Group ...'

'What about a geographical breakdown for Category Six figures. Isn't there something Jim's people can give us on that front?'

Suddenly they're all looking my way.

'Well, em ... I'll ask ... And report back.'

'OK.' The Chairperson shoots me the thinnest smile I've seen outside of a seafood counter. 'We'll minute that for circulation ahead of our next meeting.'

More bloody work! As if we all hadn't enough to do already!

The meeting finally finishes. It's 4.30 p.m. and the canteen staff have gone home. I slump into Pat's office. Pat's exact job title is unclear. I know he orders all the stationery supplies and has something to do with making sure the telephones are working. He's the guy the top brass always get to choose their Christmas cards and swap their boxy computer screens for flat ones. Pat can produce tea and sandwiches when all about him are cowed by health-and-safety regulations. Over the noise of the kettle he says, 'Cheer up, Jim lad. It may never happen.'

'Already has. I need a geographic breakdown of Category Sixes by next week. And I'm not even sure what they are.'

'Yeah, the definition is a bit dodgy. But Personnel already did a breakdown on a county-by-county basis last month. Covered all the categories separately. Just ask Sean for the bit you want, stick your name on the bottom and the job's Oxo.'

Yes, God holds us all in the palm of one hand. And amongst the fingers of the Divine Being move those few truly exceptional helpers chosen to keep on bringing order out of chaos.

new man

JOAN HANNON

See him in the kitchen, his hand gripping a solid chef's knife, chopping furiously on the thick wooden board, his heavy butcher's striped apron loosely tied around his waist, pausing only to carefully check his Nigel Slater or Jamie Oliver.

'Is it all right?' he'll anxiously enquire, as we munch our way through Pork Balls with Anchovies, or Warm Beef Salad with Mint and Rocket. 'Does it really work?' New Man asks.

I look at him and think of Older Man.

Older Man, who happily chewed his beef with onions and his pork with apple sauce, and contentedly told his wife, as he wiped his mouth, 'That was very tasty, pet.' And see New Man as he rushes downstairs, in socks and jocks, shirt in hand, hauling out the ironing board. 'I've a meeting today,' he says. 'Need the blue shirt.' Older Man – why, he couldn't use an iron. A man with an iron would burn the shirt, or himself. And if he had a meeting he needed help in selecting which of his crisply ironed shirts to wear.

Here is New Man again, in the park on Saturday morning, well-wrapped, bright-eyed baby in buggy, yawning and nodding at other New Men as they shuffle through the leaves, and stopping to exchange notes on sleep patterns and eating patterns, speech development and potty training. Older Man: 'Great little sleepers,' he'd say, 'hardly a noise out of them.' And his heavy-eyed wife would think of herself nodding over the feeding baby to the rhythmic serenade of his snoring.

But see New Man now, anxious, with a mission in mind. The races, the match. Can he go? 'Got to run it past her,' he'll say. 'Busy schedule this weekend.' And oh, see his delighted strut as he joins the throng at Croker, or Landsdowne, together with his other freed mates. Off for the day – off for the night! See him again, bleary-eyed, the next morning, as he carries the breakfast tray upstairs. Older Man: 'I'll be off,' he'd say. 'Meeting the lads at one. See you, pet.' New Man – what a species. New Woman – what a revelation.

salsa class: beginners

SHEILA KILLIAN

I can't dance, let's get that out of the way
straight away. I became a céili-failure at an
early age and missed out completely, without
regret, on the line-dancing craze. I am
neither able nor willing to follow aerobics
instructions. My school report noted 'a
general lack of physical co-ordination'. So
I'm not here to dance. Nor am I trying to
meet people, in the Limerick Garda Club
hall on a wet Wednesday night. I already
know plenty of people and don't need to

meet any more. And no, I'm not learning for a wedding, or looking for some light exercise, or planning a holiday to Cuba.

I came the first night on a dare, to keep a friend company. It was a one-night deal. I never expected to be back.

'OK, cucaracha! Dorr-two-three! Vindo-six-seven!'

The commanding words of the Lithuanian dance instructor ring out over the softer, more insidious salsa music, and we shuffle obediently to and fro on the bare boards. The few grey-haired guards at the bar are quietly amused by us: a scatter of uncoordinated women in shoes with clicky heels, and very, very few men.

We're not fast learners. We confuse our left and right, swing clockwise on the counter-clockwise turn, collide sometimes. It even took some of us ten minutes to realise 'Dorr!' and 'Vindo!' are not new, confusing salsa terms, but Lithuanian shorthand for dance towards the 'door' or 'window'. Virghinia despairs sometimes.

I find it encouraging that she is Lithuanian. Any lack of native Latin rhythm we Irish have must be multiplied for her, coming from so near to the frozen North. Yet there's no doubt that she can dance, effortlessly and stylishly. Even better, she can teach. So we shambling refugees from *Riverdance* persist, following her lead, and by the end of the night the music has taken root and here we are moving without thought to the unfamiliar rhythm. Stepping without counting, without even watching our feet. The impossibility of it all!

That's one of the things that brings us back each week, I think. The sheer improbability of it: spending a wet Limerick night learning Latin dance from a Lithuanian; salsa in the home of set dancing, under the baleful gaze of middle-aged guards.

The other thing, the big thing for me, is the music. When you spend an hour and a half moving to this music it stays. It becomes our music, so that we all head out into the dark with salsa in our heads. It makes the night look different, the shiny wet roads more interesting.

I remain uncoordinated. I still can't dance; that's not why I'm here. What I'm doing is learning a new way to listen. I listen to the music with my whole body now. I drum it in with my feet so it sticks, replaying itself automatically for days. I'm not dancing, just making a new soundtrack for the week ahead.

the readers

MICHAEL THURLOW

You pause for a second at the doorway into the room and see a scene of apparent tranquillity. The evening sun enters through panoramic windows and patio doors, a welcome if inquisitive guest, darting and dancing around the room, playing hide and seek with shadows, bouncing off mirrors and stainless steel. Outside, the world is green, rolling away from the window to trees where squirrels frisk. Inside, the room is very quiet, except for the odd creak or rustle as the two occupants move slightly every so often, for comfort, or just to ease muscles fixed in one position too long. They are reading, lost, unaware of your presence. You think to yourself, 'how peaceful'. But move closer.

The air around the boy is shimmering, a bluish tint like a force-field in a science-fiction film. Move in closer. He appears to be sitting still but now you see all the small movements he is making, as if adjusting controls. You're inside the force-field now and you realise you're on board the Starship Enterprise and the boy is Captain Kirk's First Mate. Through a porthole you can see the Earth shrinking into a tiny blue dot and you feel the excitement course through the ship as another adventure beckons. A giant black creature, with a gravelled voice, like a Welshman's the morning after they've won the Triple Crown, speaks.

'Captain, I would like to recommend that Fletcher here be awarded The Federation Medal of Honour for his heroism during the battle with the Romulans.'

You wander off to the transporter room and beam back down to Earth and you are once again standing watching the boy and, across the room, the boy's mother.

She too has left the confines of this room

and also this time zone. She is Elizabeth Bennet in *Pride and Prejudice*, terrified for her sister's good name and doubtful but hopeful that the haughty Mr Darcy can effect a rescue. Her posture changes with certain passages; stiff back, head held high, defiant, or hands wringing, fighting back tears which no man shall see. The boy's mother pictures her husband as Mr Darcy, which is extremely romantic of her, given that he is small, overweight and poverty stricken. And he'd look grotesque in a frock coat.

Elizabeth holds her hand out to be helped down from the carriage. The boy's mother raises her own hand in much the same manner, which breaks the spell. She is about to speak but you point to the boy and hold your finger to your lips. You watch him together. The shimmering of the force-field fades. He closes the book with a long sigh and a look of longing in his eyes, and you know he wishes that the adventure could last longer and that he can't wait for the next book in the series.

He sees you and his face changes. 'Hi, Dad. Can we go down to the canteen and get something to eat? I'm starving.'

Your look towards your wife is a gentle interrogation, a raised eyebrow, and her response is also silent, a tiny lift of the shoulder. You take the handles of the boy's wheelchair, release the brake and the three of you trundle off, leaving the ward apparently empty. But look closer.

derby and me

GER PETRIE

You sit down heavily across the kitchen table.

'Good morning,' I say.

Your brow knits a ploughed furrow as you stick your head into the cereal box.

'Where did you find this? Triple Berries! You'd need a garda search and rescue team to locate any berries in here.'

'Grumble, grouse, growl,' I want to say. I refrain.

'It's a new one. I thought you'd like to try it for a change.'

'What was wrong with the other one, Special X or whatever it's called? Why change a good thing? At least, now and then, I could see a bit of fruit in that.'

I switch off. You, Mr Pickahole, are starting off your day as you mean to go on. You, Mr Pickahole, recently retired Managing Director, having browbeaten your staff into running your business for forty years, are now directing your ire at me, staff of one.

'You said there was no post yesterday.'

'Grouch, gripe, moan.' It's only a fleeting thought in my mind.

'That's right, I checked the box yesterday evening. It was empty.'

'No, it wasn't. There were several letters. You only peered into the top. You need to open the box with the key to check it properly. That's how I discovered it was full.'

'Whinge, whine, bleat.' My lips don't move. I close my ears again. The silence in my head is very pleasant. I notice your mouth is on the move once more. I open a small perceptive channel.

'You left the gas on last night when you went to your writing class. It was hissing away for two hours after you left. It's a miracle I'm still here. How I wasn't blown into the next life I'll never know.'

'PITY YOU WEREN'T!' Did I really

say that out loud? I glance across the table at you. Your expression confirms I most certainly did. God, I'm getting very brave. Daring and dauntless now, I continue.

'As and from today there is a new rule in this marriage. You, Mr Pickahole, will be allowed a maximum of four complaints per day. It's 9.30 a.m. and as you have lodged three and half faults so far, I'd be very selective, if I were you, for the remainder of the day. Perhaps something particularly serious may turn up and need to be remonstrated.'

Your mouth is open very wide. My auditory range is tuned up to full power. The steady tick of the kitchen clock is the only sound between us.

the staff do

CATHY SWEENEY

The hotel bristles with festivity as I approach.
All around are lights and sparkle and laughter.
I heave myself from the car, battling down
vague dread as I clatter up the stone steps and
swing through the door and into the eye of
the foyer. I can see no one I know. Chirpy
uniformed staff intervene and I am ushered
towards the mulled-wine reception.

Nothing is allowed interfere with the
mood of absolute enjoyment. I down the
hot cloying wine at breakneck speed as my

co-workers collect around me. We are a tightly knit group of relative strangers. We laugh and joke together, exhibiting outward signs of bonding to distinguish ourselves from other work tribes.

A bell rings us into dinner. A loud and rather persistent bell. The staff are experts. They troop out with military precision. A weary waitress leans forcefully into my ear. 'Turkey and Ham or Salmon?' I butter my roll and eat the soup and think momentarily of a nursing home. I eye the waitress desperately, willing her to pour the wine. Steady, steady, I think as I drain another glass.

'Where's your hat?' A colleague screeches at me half-accusingly. There is no middle way here. I fix a ridiculous hat of the variety worn by show monkeys to my head and smile.

At the next table a group of IT consultants are blowing into their paper whistles like referees calling full time at an All-Ireland match. I think about lip reading as I struggle to respond appropriately to the woman beside me. Over the din and the whistles I catch every third word she says. I need to go to the loo but the chairs are sandwiched together too tightly. The heat is overbearing and I strip down to my black Lycra top. My make-up feels greasy.

Dessert arrives and with it comes Santa. My jaw is tired from smiling. Kriskindle. We all clap. Shrieks of laughter greet the blow-up doll and innuendoes fly as a new girl is given massage oil. The band kicks off with a throbbing rendition of 'Waterloo'. People leap up to dance. I squeeze out and head for the loo. On my way back I get lost and stumble through a 'Staff Only' entrance. A waiter guides me back to the function room with the patience of a benign parent. I talk over the music telling people things I've been keeping to myself for months. A gaggle of younger women pull me up to dance. We form a circle and mime the words.

For the first time in ages I wonder am I old. I wonder if my bra is giving enough support. Finally the music fades out and I scurry off the dancefloor. I scan the table for my drink but find only stains and used napkins. The younger ones arrive back and order shots. I slip my jacket from the back of the chair and head for the door, forgetting my good scarf and scented Kriskindle candle. And then it is all over for another year and I am out in the still silent night air of mid-December.

the bedsit

TRISH BYRNE

I stood on the bottom step with the other hopeless-looking hopefuls, ready to view the bedsit. I was determined to cut myself off. I would leave him and go to live by myself, in splendid isolation, here on Bloomfield Avenue. I would make a new, smaller life that meant answering the phone only if I felt like it, eating an orange and some ice cream for dinner if I wanted and never tripping over broken bike lights again. It would be a neat and compact life. I could frame photos of my brothers without having to match them with pictures of his sisters or gap-toothed nieces and nephews. I could listen to my music all the time, watch soap operas in bed, go for little walks, ignore the neighbours, come home drunk and sleep in my clothes.

It was my turn to view. 'It's only for one,' the landlady reminded me, as if I had a football team hidden downstairs, ready to move in as soon as her back was turned. The room itself put paid to any ideas like that. It wasn't so much a room as a walled-off bit of hallway that held a single bed as narrow as a school ruler, a wardrobe that blocked half of the room's only window and a rickety old plant stand where the telly was obviously supposed to go. About two inches past the foot of the bed, the nylon carpet gave way to lino, indicating the start of the kitchen. A sink and cooker fought each other for space under shelves so old they groaned even though they were empty. A thin wall and single door separated all this from the shower-room. Shower, sink and toilet were so close together that they appeared to overlap.

'We like quiet tenants here,' said the landlady.

'You'd have to,' I said. All around me I could hear television voices keeping the other tenants company while they heated their beans or fried their sausages. Instead of a smell of cabbage, there seemed to be a permanent scent of curry powder in the air. I shivered to think of the kind of life I would have here. It wasn't what I'd planned when I decided to make a break for it.

I knew that all I had to do was go home to him and say nothing. He didn't know I was leaving. He need never know I had ever thought about it. I could drink a bottle of wine and tell my girlfriends about it and we might all agree that I'd almost made a terrible mistake.

I couldn't help stretching as I reached the front door again. It was good to be back outside and free of such a suffocating place. The evening air was warm and welcoming and I walked by the canal for a while, alone. I could start again tomorrow.

while they are retired

ANONYMOUS

The battle is over, but not the war. The client sits mute, head bowed nearly to his knees, sweaty hands clasped. Never a man for ties, the one I ordered him to wear is pulled loose. I will insist it be tightened to his neck when the buzzer tells us the jury are returning – even if asking does remind me of the last act of a hangman. The girlfriend, ever present through the ordeal, has her arm about his shoulder as she too leans forward, whispering unheard encouragements. I know the prosecutor well, so we discourse lightly as we too wait. Just like footballers from neighbouring villages might banter once the match is over, counsel allow themselves this break, although the outcome is yet to be determined. If there is a conviction both must resume positions on opposite sides.

Innocent or guilty, he is now in custody. The client asks the garda on duty can he leave the courtroom to have a cigarette. I follow him out.

'Well, somebody in there is rooting for you!' He manages a wan smile, his hand shaking so hard the fag can hardly find his mouth.

So – did he do it? Swore blind to me he didn't. Swore blind to the jury he didn't, that another in the group of foul-mouthed, spaced-out youths outside the pub threw the bottle that left the girl with a bad gash on her head.

She now sat chewing gum, fidgeting with her hair, her bracelet, her watch. An arrogant look, I thought, but then don't I always? She identified him as did two others. One girl who proclaimed she saw him do it ('Yeah, sure, yeah') had had two pint glasses of something called a 'fat frog' – green, apparently; three measures of spirit per pint.

My client had but one witness – an odd

man, but a sober man, walking by on his way home who says he can't be sure it wasn't my man but thinks the assailant was taller and is sure he had a beard. My man didn't shave his off before the trial. Moral dilemma: should I have asked him to? Anyway I didn't.

Back in the courtroom we sit. Twenty minutes. The buzzer sounds. Verdict. 'Your tie!' We all assemble our dignities and positions.

'All rise!' His Lordship sits. The jury files in. Inscrutable. Damn. 'Have you reached a verdict upon which you are all agreed? Just answer yes – or no.'

'Yes.' The issue paper is opened, and the verdict read aloud.

old brown eyes

ANNE MOLLOY

I'll never forget those eyes. Never, as long as
I live. They were so very brown. I just can't
look away. They are mesmerising, soulful,
doleful, bovine eyes. I wait for the spark of
humour, the dawn of a twinkle, a wink, the
twitching birth of a grin, the punch line.
But they don't change, no movement, no
wavering, just liquid, rheumy, gazing, big,
brown eyes. They don't seem to match his
greying hair. I wonder what he looked like
when he was young, his hair perhaps a
lustrous, rich chestnut brown.

I wish my legs weren't dangling like a two-year-old's. I wish I had my shoes on, that they weren't tucked neatly a few feet beneath me. It feels somewhat undignified; I feel at a disadvantage, vulnerable. I want to stand up. I want to look away from those big brown eyes.

Why is the other guy so still, so quiet? It's not a funeral. Is he the apprentice, learning the tricks of the trade? Is he intent on listening, witnessing the master at work in order not to miss a single miniscule gem of wisdom? Will he have learnt something today? I want to drag my gaze away from old brown eyes to look at him, at those bright pink blotches the size and shape of an old 50p coin on each angular, bony cheek. I want to look at the glasses planted heavily on the bridge of his narrow, pointed nose, at those hungry eyes behind them, the size of saucers. We could have a giggle, him and I, at how serious the old master is being.

I can see the lips below those brown eyes moving, working, mouthing. Can't really make out what he is saying – blah blah … MRI … scan … echo echo. Still no sparkle, still no twitching at the corners of the mouth.

I wonder if he's married. Does she still love to bathe, to wallow in those beautiful chocolatey pools, or has she learnt to hate their sadness, their seriousness, their inscrutability, their apparent indifference? Does he look at her like this; has all feeling, all emotion, been liquefied through years of repetition, of inevitability, of correctness, of illness … of bearing bad news?

I really have to go. I'm meeting Emer in Bray to help her plan her new kitchen. It will take me at least half an hour to get there. I'm already late. So get on with it. What are those bulbous, bulging, bleary eyes trying to convey? They're really annoying me now, and my feet are getting cold. The room is closing in on me. I am finding it a little difficult to breathe. My heart is pounding, rattling at my rib cage. I need to go to the loo.

MRI scans are for people who are ill; they don't squander their supposedly meagre funds on maybes. I know — I'm not stupid. I'm in a rush. Echo, echo, echo, neurological irregularity, blah blah … typical symptoms … echo, disturbance … central nervous system … blah blah, echo echo … echo … Oh, spit it out, Old Brown Eyes!

the small town

CAROLE ZABBAL

It was the way there was never enough space for everyone to sit comfortably, with Feargal's sister often perched on the armrest of the sofa, and the fact that even a year on, I was still given the largest chair by the fireside, treated like an honoured guest.

It was the way that conversation always felt stilted, strained and shoved around until it would return, inexorably, to the neighbour's new car or that poor woman who died in a car accident in Mullingar. And it was also the indescribable tedium, the days stretching out interminably, marked only by the one o'clock news, the kids' cartoons, the angelus.

It was the way I dared not refuse the endless cups of tea and biscuits, and the way the same plate of mashed potatoes and vegetables arrived at dinner week after week. I still raised eyebrows in the small town, because I was a vegetarian, an atheist and had committed the absurdity of spending eighteen years in schooling when I could have been working. It was because I wasn't born or raised there: a blow-in. I did not like the small town.

It could have been any small town to me, anywhere that wasn't a city. Far from the quaint thatched-cottage countryside I'd visited as a tourist. But despite the sins and thrills of Dublin, where we now lived, his smile was never bigger than when he went home to his family at the weekend. He fervently, vigorously loved his hometown. And I, well, I loved a man from a small town, and eventually I learned the names of all his family's neighbours and their extended relations.

And by the time I had learned that Mrs Tierney's sister had a farm with horses years ago where Feargal and the kids of the estate used to play, and that old Mr Ward next door, the second person on the estate to get a telephone, used to call for Feargal's mammy when her firstborn Paddy called from Amsterdam, the most unlikely thing had happened.

The town had grown on me, slowly, inconspicuously. I started to see surreptitious kindnesses and silent bonds, the lifeblood of the small town, like the neighbour with the new car who would give lifts to his elderly neighbours at all hours of the day.

It was also about then that I lost my job in Dublin, and idle gossip in the local turned to heartfelt concerns, followed by phone calls with leads on vacancies in the small town. Sure wouldn't this be a great time to move 'home' anyway?

And as for the tea, well, instead of sitting watching the news and gobbling biscuits, I was being asked to make it when the neighbours came round.

I had graduated to the armrest.

bread

JIM CLARKEN

I bake. I am not ashamed to admit to it. It
may all sound very post-Celtic Tiger, in a
country that has gone baking mad, where
the new black is not pink, but a golden-
brown, crusty colour. Despite this current
fashion, baking is not without its drawbacks.
The main one is the health-food shop itself.
The dash past posters advertising Angel
Workshops, the ducking under wind-chimes
so my bald crown won't set them off and the
sidestepping around dream-catchers with

feathers that tickle the ears. There are also the leaflets advertising pilates, tai chi, yoga and reiki classes. I'm there for the flour, a top-shelf commodity at the back of the shop that comes in ever-increasing varieties: pasta, Zero-Zero, strong, unbleached.

As I reach for a bag of flour I sometimes feel guilty, in a smug sort of way. 'Cause I have a secret that all you people struggling with your brand new books on baking should know but won't. There is no mention of it in most baking tomes with their beautifully photographed breads and cakes. These books, after all, are not intended for use but for display.

I started to bake ten years ago when the dole dictated how much I got to eat each week. It was a bleak time and I learned, among other things, that one bag of flour and a sachet of yeast went a long way, breadwise. This discovery led me to become an accidental baker.

Most new bakers out there are probably going through what I went through – the small-yellow-loaf stage of yeast baking. Eat this bread, enjoy it, it has its merits. But there are places to go if you persist.

Ten years ago I had no options so I persisted. I learned to knock back dough, to shape it, to wait. Gradually things improved.

True, my breads were still misshapen and stunted but they lost their livery yellow look. I now bake jaundice-free croissants, bread rolls and panettone. I can now afford bread but I still bake. I bake for the crust, for the taste, for the ingredients I know go into my breads, real butter for instance. But how did I make the transition from worthy effort to mouth-watering breads?

My breakthrough came not from any book, but from a magazine article by a real baker, of real breads. It was from him I heard of the crucial ingredients, the secrets kept from the amateur. It was from him I heard of Ferment and of Steam. So save yourself five years in the baking wilderness. Ferment and Steam.

the mouths of babes

MARY BARBER

The words from the back seat ripped through me. I didn't know that a child could be so cruel, that their words could cause so much pain.

'Yes, Mam, we'd prefer if you went back to work and Gwen could mind us all the time.'

This simple statement rocked my whole world. I had never wanted to work full time *and* have children. It had worked out that way for a while, but now I had achieved my dream and was at home with my kids. I was just getting used to the whole housework thing and felt really sure that everything was working out for the best.

But now my four-year-old daughter had undermined my whole reason for being, and when I asked the two-year-old what she felt on the matter, she rowed in with her older sister. They definitely would both prefer if I was working every day and they could be with Gwen – all day.

The rain poured down outside and the wipers struggled to clear it. They seemed to reflect how my mind struggled with the emotions flooding in. But on I drove, bringing my girls back to our house. The house that we had endeavoured to make into a real home for our family. The compromises we had made, the things we had given up, because we thought it was best for children if they were reared by their parents.

But this philosophy obviously didn't sit too well with our children. Am I a bad mother? Where have I gone wrong?

And so the argument ran through my head. It festered and boiled inside me. The times when I thought, 'No, it's just childish foolishness from a pre-schooler.' And then the thoughts: 'I'll show those ungrateful children. I will go back to work full time, but I'll get a Nanny in – that'll show them who is boss around here!'

My husband told me I was blowing it out of proportion. But I had been hurt in a way that few, if any, had ever managed to hurt me. And I picked away at that wound, trying to get an explanation from the children or get them to expand on their reasons for wanting me off the scene.

A few nights later, I was sitting in bed with my four-year-old. As she searched for Wally, she just casually said, 'I actually don't want you to back to work, Mam.' My breath stopped and again I was flooded with emotion. Now I could know peace again. This child of mine held my life in her hands and she didn't even know it. And as we continued to look for Wally, the only thing I could manage to say was an insubstantial, 'I love you.'

to oz and back

SHARON VOGIATZI

The prodigal daughter has returned to the
family home, head hung in shame. The I-
told-you-so glances bounce off my forehead.
I signal for my brother to help unload the
car. It's bursting with memorabilia from
Spain, where I met my husband and lived
not-so-happily-ever-after.

My old home stands before me, its
shadow enveloping me in a sense of failure.
I stop in the doorway and repeat the mantra,
'There's no place like home.' Who am I
trying to convince?

I climb the stairs with a heavy heart and enter my bedroom. A painted rainbow arches across one side of the room and I wonder if I've been searching for gold in all the wrong places.

The sadness is overwhelming. I cannot stay still with my cutting memories so I decide to spring-clean before moving in. Silly school-girl letters and Brad Pitt posters are stuffed into a large plastic bag, along with a pair of size eight jeans. Gone are the days of make-believe and a tiny waist!

The next couple of hours are spent poring over a collection of diaries written religiously from my tenth through to my nineteenth year. The first journal boasts curling pages filled with a belief that everything would work out in the end. Boys were disgusting, your mother was your role model and friends were always there for you. There was a kind of innate wisdom in that.

I move on to the handwritten sequels which tell of unrequited love, a first, muddled kiss and a virginity lost, never to be found again.

My aching knees bring me back to the present. I, reluctantly and self-destructively, open the wedding wardrobe. The dress stares accusingly out at me. The photo album begs to be touched. I leaf through happy pictures filled with flowers and shining eyes. My tears fall onto the pages like rain on a window pane.

I feel as though I'm being torn in two. I've had enough. I shouldn't be alone with my loneliness. It might suffocate me when no one's watching. The wound is too fresh and the tears too salty.

I walk downstairs and wonder how many mothers open the door to find her daughter, laden down with suitcases, crying the song of her woe, 'I'm home!'

I walk into the kitchen and my mother asks, 'Tea?'

cowardice

L. HINGERTY

I am stuck at the traffic lights when I recognise her walk. Although it is December, she is strolling along in a floppy skirt, her bare legs still light brown, left over from a faded summer. Her shoes are ready for the bin, but her elegance makes up for them.

She tosses back her beautiful hair, a deep chestnut, and I am furious to feel that little lurch hop somewhere between my heart and chest. She crosses the road without looking, her olive-skinned face mischievous.

Carrying several library books – she must be heading for home. All she needs for the holidays is in her arms.

I could go round the block once more along the sea route. That road is one-way but I might catch her at the other end if the lights are green this time … I could stop and say, 'Hi, Carla, would you like a lift?'

No, she is too near her little house.

'Hi, want to go for coffee?'

But I've already had two strong ones and the anxiety is showing in the shaky movements of the steering wheel. Maybe if I stopped she would just open the door and get in. We could have a chat. Where are those cigarettes?

There she is, in the village, coming out of the grocer. I could wave. Beep the horn maybe. She is carrying a bag full of fruit. She looks up, with a ready smile and her hand half-raised in the air. To wave she would have to carry fruit and books with one hand.

The look of hurt is an age that shadows her prettiness. She drops her arm and passes the books back to her other hand. Her walk changes as she crosses the road, this time looking where she is going. I notice this from the rear-view mirror as my courage drains away.

I drive on.

the key

MARGARET MCCARTHY

Soon, too soon, we will return each other's keys. Our neighbours of thirteen years are moving. Without that key I am sure to run out of milk at least twice a week, so from now on black tea and coffee are on the cards for unexpected visitors.

When we, with our three children, took occupation of No. 60 there was a lovely young couple living in No. 59. As the years passed two beautiful girls were born. Our girls would babysit and I could let myself quietly in to ensure all was well.

Our key was always available in No. 59. Family and extended family on both sides knew there was always a key 'next door'. Now how our dog found out about the key is a mystery, but it became his habit that when he couldn't gain admission to No. 60 he would bark outside No. 59 until our key was used to let him in at home.

When necessary, heat was turned on for returning travellers, each other's dogs were fed and walked, windows opened and closed, helping hands available to strip old wallpaper, scones, apple tarts and chocolate cake shared, grass cut, trees trimmed and impromptu barbecues held on nice summer days. Joys and sorrows were shared over cups of tea. It was almost like we were all the one family.

The 'For Sale' sign is up and people are viewing. Everything will change for both families. We will miss them and we wish them well.

When the keys are finally handed over we know that they meant much more than easy access. It was real mutual trust, friendship, love and a happy, easy-shared living. Whoever moves in will not replace you, and all at No. 60 say 'thanks for all the memories'.

the gallery

Michael Minihan

If I ever go missing, the first place the search party would look is the National Gallery. They know who I am. I'm the young fella they have to chase out at closing time most days. Anyway, there aren't many art bores in their early twenties so I stick out like a missing ear.

For a little while, some people are even attracted to art bores. Take this girl I met not so long ago on the number fourteen bus, for example. One summer evening, after getting my fine-art fix at the museum, she sat down beside me on the top deck and gave me the ins and outs on every picture she could think of in the gallery. I was taken by her. Somehow, it was as if she knew that name-dropping the masters was the way to my heart. She reeled them off like they were her close acquaintances and I was hooked. By the top of the Rathmines Road, I had asked her out. By Rathgar, I was deeply infatuated. Whoever said that a twenty-three-year-old art bore had no chance in love?

For her twenty-first birthday, I booked tickets to the Hermitage exhibition in London but she declined the offer.

'Why?' I asked. 'Is it too soon?'

'No,' she replied. 'It's because I can't spend another minute listening to how much you love Caravaggio, Rembrandt and Van Gogh. You bore me, Michael. I'm sorry.'

I was stunned. Particularly as she pro-nounced Van Gogh with a sharp second 'g'. Art lover indeed. She had been faking it all that time. My mother says it will happen again so it was good preparation. I look back on it now and say, Botticelli had Venus; I had Veronica. Oh, and the Hermitage exhibition was amazing, by the way.

night into morning

SHEILA MAHER

As my feet hit the cold kitchen floor, I wish I had remembered to put on socks. I shiver as I fill the kettle and stand hugging myself tightly, waiting for it to boil. I stare out the window and can just make out the black and bare outline of trees in the back garden. It is still dark outside – there isn't even a hint of dawn breaking in the distance. I know I looked at my watch only a minute or two ago, but I have already forgotten what time it is. It's very early, of that I'm sure.

I look around at the mess in the kitchen and try to forget all of the work that still has to be done to make this home habitable. How could everything have changed so completely in one short year?

Our postal code has increased by ten, our mortgage has doubled, our income has halved, we have two gardens instead of one. Our sex life has quartered, then quartered again. Instead of eight hours' sleep I'm lucky if I get five; instead of several nights out a week we can barely drag ourselves out for one. We are three instead of two.

Only the briefest while ago, I used to pity the two-car, two-kid suburbanites whose days seemed so dull and routine. I would wonder how and why people chose to exist like that while we were really living!

I can hear her cries getting more insistent, so I will the kettle along. As it comes to the boil I pour the bubbling water around the bottle and make my way upstairs. My legs are heavy and my back stiff – they could do with another hour or two of rest. I glance at our bedroom door and think of my side of the bed, still warm and snug with my shape pressed into it, and a fuzzy heat emanating from him. Unfortunately I'm not going to be able to take up that position again for some time.

I flick on the light in her bedroom and immediately the crying stops and instead her legs and arms start flapping excitedly. As I look into the cot, a broad gummy smile cracks on her face. My insides swell to bursting point. Is it me or the anticipation of her bottle that has her so happy? I reach in to pick her up. *This* is my favourite part of the day. This is when I reacquaint myself with her wriggling body and gorgeous smell. This is life.

Our day begins.

the student party

DYLAN BRADLEY

I rap my knuckles against the wooden door of Flat 14. It has a tattered banner across it that reads 'The party is here'. I've only been at college two weeks, and already I feel tired of this sort of get-together. The banner is tattered because they used it last Sunday as well.

The door swings open. My friends and I walk in and the air of desperation hits me like a cold boot in the face. There's a cheap cake on the table and four or five balloons are stuck to the presses. Placebo is on the radio and everyone starts talking to each another in monotone, mostly trying to find common ground. Nobody does and we start talking about the weather.

The girls talk about a disco they went to last weekend and the guys talk about the upcoming Ireland match. I feel like turning around and running away screaming, but I stay quiet. The girls are dressed up as if they're going out. I ask one of the dark-haired ones where they're going and she says that she's already there. This evokes such a strong sense of sorrow that I actually wince and look away.

Then a thought occurred to me that I never had before. Since when did people refer to sitting in a room with dull music talking about things that don't matter to people you don't know as a party anyway? Who was the first person to get away with doing that? And why is it that, as a nation, all we have to do in the realm of fun is to sit in someone's house or go to the same disco again?

To make a long story short, I voiced my protest and some responded by telling me that this *was* fun. So, I grabbed a piece of cheap cake and I let myself out.

the salon

HELEN DELANEY

Blonde is the new black. Everywhere you go: blonde streaks, blonde highlights, dark, light and white blonde. Young ones with home dye jobs that look awful. Well-paid preppie types in their twenties with expensive salon jobs. And it's spreading. Forties, fifties, sixties, no one is going grey any more: they're going blonde. Ten women in the salon and six with blonde tresses. Who do they think they're kidding? And what about natural blondes, don't they have copyright or something?

My own locks fit with the rest of me. Rich brown and shiny like a chestnut, maybe a middle-aged and slightly pissed-off chestnut. Brunette à la the old American movies, with a bit of natural curl. A natural curl had value once; now those without can buy it at the hairdressers. I've no grey but when I do I'm not going to fight it. Someone has to make a stand. I stare at my reflection.

The stylist has shoulder-length black with blonde streaks on top. Ho hum. At least she's not middle-aged, probably in her early twenties. It's the trendy punk look, right?

'Did you ever think of getting some highlights?' She looks gloomily at my wet brown head.

I'm non-committal. 'What do you suggest?'

'Well, it's coming up to Christmas, so rich plums and deep purples are seasonal.'

The stylist, like most in the salon, is young and female. Black anything is the unofficial official uniform. She's in dark satin skin-tight jeans with a tight polyester top revealing generous cleavage and hugging only some of her expanding waistline, which spills over the front of her jeans. Skinny, slim and pleasantly plump or pregnant, acres of waistline is the fashion. I wonder if it'll be a spring baby.

'It won't be long now!' I chirp merrily,

eyeing her widening midriff in the mirror in front. She glares at me angrily. 'Till what?' Well, perhaps not. 'Till Christmas,' I reply weakly, thanking God silently that it's October.

She doesn't look convinced as she chops aggressively at my boringly brown hair. I need a distraction. 'Do you think I should go for some highlights?' The chopping stops abruptly. Her eyes land warmly on mine. She even looks happy. I'm a nice person again. She heads off to get the colour chart.

My brown head looks accusingly back at me but I'm distracted. I can't knock the girl back twice in one visit. Maybe just a bit of plum.

observations

MYLES CHRISTIAN

The place is quite grotty really. Funny, I hadn't noticed before. Is it because this is a new situation for me? On my own in a pub. Watching. Like being on the top of a bus. You see more.

I get some funny looks. Sitting in a corner, pint in front of me, scribbling furiously in the small notebook that has become my constant companion since I took up writing. The observer being observed.

There are regulars here, of course. The

man who always sits alone, by a side wall, earphones on, eyes closed, listening to a Walkman. His attention divided between the sound in his ears and the drink by his side. Two pints of lager, one full, the other half drunk. I wonder if he is an optimist or a pessimist.

A couple, maybe sixty-something, sit across from me – he with the comb-over hairstyle, she with her arm protectively through the straps of her ample handbag, Thatcher-like. They sit stoically side by side, eyes to the front, conversation zero, enduring each other for the sake of a jar. Sad, I think. Whatever happened to communication?

The young couple with eyes only for each other – I christen them Budweiser and Smirnoff Ice. Her hand rests lightly on his knee, his arm flows casually around the back of the seat. They talk and talk. Will they sit stoically, side by side, enduring each other's company in forty years from now? I hope not.

Some of the lounge staff are new, some I know quite well, but multinational they certainly are. Like the lad from some far-eastern place. 'What's his name?' I'd asked a barman once. 'Wallace. He likes to be called Wallace. *Braveheart* and all that, you know.

His favourite.' 'Oh,' I said. I remember we'd had to teach him basic English that first time.

'Vodka, slim-line white and a pint of Guinness.' The puzzled look. 'VOD-KA.' This in a slightly raised voice. Why do we assume foreigners are deaf? Volume does not speak volumes.

I taste my pint. Beautiful. The man who invented Guinness should be canonised. I lose my train of thought, take another sip and look around. God, the place really is grotty. Smoke-stained ceiling, beer-stained floor. I feel like the filling in some filthy sandwich.

I look at the clock. Its impassive face stares back. Both of us passing time, though it is me doing the waiting.

A movement catches my eye. A flash of colour in the drab surroundings. A 'young-wan', looks about sixteen, heading to the ladies'. Red dress. The air of a half-forgotten Chris de Burgh song plays its way into my thoughts. I wonder if she knows the song. Probably not. Too young.

Another movement. Ah, here she is. About time. 'What'll ya have, love? Vodka and slim-line? Wallace,' I call, 'Vodka and white and another pint please.'

My Godot has arrived.

the journey

MARY MCGREGOR

Standing on the ship, peering through the mist at the faint rocky peak, I feel like an American. A large black suitcase on wheels, a guidebook of Scotland, the neatly drawn family tree that directed me to this place, a lump in my throat – all present and correct. Only the blue rinse and the plaid trousers are missing. In a way, I'm embarrassed. Isn't half the world trying to prove their Irishness? I am Irish, but I feel something else too, though I don't know why. Perhaps it started in college.

'Mary McGregor?' The forty-something registrar read my signature curiously. 'Really?'

'Yeah.'

'Torn between two lovers?' she asked.

'What?'

'Feeling like a fool?'

She started to sing, as I looked on, mystified.

'There was a singer by that name.'

'Oh right … never heard of her,' I said, grabbing my student card and getting away from the crooning official as fast as I could.

These days very few people burst into song at the mere mention of my name. Now I'm more likely to get a poor impression of Liam Neeson's turn as the famous Highland outlaw in *Rob Roy*.

'Yore say good tae me, Maaary MacGraygor.'

'Oh aye, right enough, so ah am,' I'd reply in my best Billy Connolly.

Perhaps Billy was my inspiration. On his tour of Britain and Ireland, he stood amongst a pile of stones in Connemara and proudly, without sarcasm or irony, announced that this was his great-grandfather's house. Had it been anyone else, Billy would have shown no mercy. 'It's a pile of stones, ye stupid bugger!'

So here I am on the Isle of Arran, trying

to find my great-grandfather's pile of stones. I feel more emotional than I expected as I step onto the dock. My breathing stops for a moment as I look toward the peak of Goatfell standing like a mighty cathedral high above Brodick Bay.

I hire a car and head north along the coast road. I don't ask for directions. I already know the way, though not by the divine inspiration of my ancestors – I have been studying this map for a year. Arran is Scotland in miniature, and these are the Highlands. My stomach lurches as the car crests a peak and descends at forty-five degrees. It's so beautiful, I can't think why my great-grandfather left.

'You can't eat scenery,' says the West of Ireland in me. Hardship is proportional to beauty, and I know it must have been hard here.

I cross the bridge and turn right into the graveyard at Clachan. Trees and a stream protect one side of the burial ground. I walk amongst the graves until I catch sight of a name as familiar as my own, because it is my own. The first descendant of John McGregor of Shiskine, Isle of Arran has come home, and I understand the crazy Americans for the first time.

the end of the day

D. WOODS

I remember him when he was younger.
Dapper in his blazers and striking cravats,
always just that bit unusual, given the rest of
us in our jeans and baggy jumpers. Further-
more, although he was a conservative
Catholic compared to our 'save the world'
ideals, he was a worthy conversationalist. And
I looked forward to meeting him in the city-
centre hotel where he had a permanent
room close to the street where he was born.
He thought he would end his days among

the people he knew. On Saturday nights in the hotel bar there were great parties and sing-songs, and of course lashings of food laid on by the ardent owners who loved the convivial atmosphere.

One cold November Remembrance Sunday I met him on the way to St Patrick's Cathedral for the first ecumenical march by the Irish army in their blue berets following the UN flag. But it was he who reminisced about the Irishmen who had taken the king's shilling and fought in the British army. And the fights, with poppy-sellers being thrown into the Liffey because the ceremony was the prerogative of the Royal British Legion.

But all of that was to change. The EEC became the EU. The pound changed to euro and the distaste of king's shilling faded with the swish of the Celtic Tiger's tail. The hotel passed from father to son and he was suddenly moved with his few possessions to a care hospital for elderly gentlemen. All of this happened at Christmas, a busy time at best, and he got lost in the confusion.

Gone were the days of his spick and span clothes and witty conversation. In their place is a shell of a man. The people who knew and saluted him have gone their separate ways. But I continued the attachment, hoping to take him for drives around his favourite haunts or at least walk the hospital grounds. Gradually, as his hearing declined into a deafness no hearing aid could cure and his physical being became more infirm, I began to carry a jotter to communicate. Finally, however, I had to accept his frailty and the absurdity of my own situation.

Now I visit on Sundays, usually between his dinner and tea, and occasionally I find him asleep. Last week the nurses told me he had taken a turn and I checked to make sure they had my number, just in case. But I continue to make my calls, difficult as they are, until he is no more among us. Because he was then, and still is now, my friend.